Organisationa

C000226084

This book provides a guide to navigating the paradoxical tensions of organisational resilience and presents a framework to aid individuals and businesses to become more open-minded, flexible, and mindful in managing the unexpected.

The book offers the reader pragmatic and insightful means to achieve a 'state' of organisational resilience, making use of current research data that shows how managers anticipate and respond to actual and near-miss incidents. Grounded in the day-to-day reality of managers, the goal of this book is to offer a unique theoretical framework as a platform for practical application for the improvement of organisational outcomes. It provides insights into ten key capabilities that enable the reader to set up a successful program of organisational resilience, taking a cross-cutting approach and focusing on implementation while having solid foundations in theory.

This is an ideal book for advanced students and executive education courses in risk management, crisis management, and business continuity, as well as thoughtful practitioners.

Dr Elmar Kutsch is Associate Professor in Risk Management at Cranfield University, School of Management, UK.

Organisational Resilience

Navigating Paradoxical Tensions

 **Elmar Kutsch**

 Routledge
Taylor & Francis Group

LONDON AND NEW YORK

Designed cover image: © Getty Images

First published 2023
by Routledge
4 Park Square, Milton Park, Abingdon, Oxon OX14 4RN

and by Routledge
605 Third Avenue, New York, NY 10158

Routledge is an imprint of the Taylor & Francis Group, an informa business

British Library Cataloguing-in-Publication Data
A catalogue record for this book is available from the British Library

ISBN: 978-0-367-53732-6
ISBN: 978-0-367-53731-9
ISBN: 978-1-003-08311-5

DOI: 10.4324/9781003083115

Typeset in Times New Roman
by codeMantra

Contents

Figures

Tables

Boxes

Foreword

We find ourselves in a time of unprecedented challenges. Climate change, biodiversity loss, global pandemic, political uncertainty, social change, economic turbulence, and rapid digitalisation will transform all communities, sectors, and societies in the coming decades. Negotiating these challenges and the wicked trade-offs required is essential if we are to secure the long-term resilience of our organisations, communities, cities, and societies.

The COVID-19 pandemic highlighted the tensions inherent in resilience. The primary instrument of containment was used to protect health services and save lives, yet lockdowns led to large gross domestic product contractions that had adverse impacts and pushed up inequalities in the labour market, household living standards, mental health, and wealth. The solution to wicked problems, like lives vs livelihoods, can never be right or wrong because stakeholders will always have competing perspectives.

Organisations of all types face resilience tensions and paradoxes. Every organisation must mitigate risk through compliance and a prescriptive system of rules, regulations, and standards whilst at the same time they need the ability to respond rapidly to emergent problems and formulate creative solutions. Similarly, organisations need to meet productivity and efficiency goals and delivery more from less to remain competitive, whilst at the same time, they need to innovate to keep pace with technology, business models, and consumer trends. Resilience isn't only about responding to disruptions and surviving in adversity but seeking opportunities and ensuring the organisation is fit for the future.

As we move beyond the COVID crisis into the new world that lies ahead, we have a once-in-a-lifetime opportunity to re-write the rules, reimagine resilience, and explore fresh, exciting possibilities within a very different business climate. The most successful organisations in the new world will be those that are able to adapt quickly yet thoughtfully to what is coming.

This book examines how business leaders, policymakers, and other decision-makers can address current and future challenges and build resilience by managing tensions and paradoxes. Drawing on the very latest research thinking and practical case examples, the book makes a significant contribution to the theory and practice of organisational resilience.

David Denyer
Professor of Leadership and Organizational Change
Head, ORaCL, Organizational Resilience and Change Leadership Group
Lead for the Cranfield University Resilience Grand Challenge
Strategic Business Director

Chapter 1

Towards a paradox mindset

In pursuit of reliable performance

The odds are stacked against us! We inevitably face the prospect of adversity that may derail our well-laid plans and undermine our ability to maintain reliable performance:

> Reliability has become a worldwide watchword of citizens, clients, leaders, and executives. For some, reliability means constancy of service; for others, the safety of core activities and processes (Laporte, 1996). Increasingly, it means both anticipation and resilience, the ability of organisations to plan for shocks as well as to absorb and rebound from them in order to provide services safely and continuously.
>
> (Roe and Schulman, 2008, p. 5)

Fortunately, the threat of unreliable performance that could climax in a crisis or irrecoverable disaster, is signalled by two types of incidents: near-misses and accidents.

Broadly speaking, a near-miss, colloquially referred to as near-hits, close calls, or even good catches, constitutes an unplanned, undesired circumstance, condition, or actual event that has the potential to adversely affect reliable performance, resulting in harm, injury, damage, loss, or the incompletion of a task; but ultimately it did not do so.

In contrast, an accident is an undesirable happening having a considerable, tangible adverse effect on reliable performance. The term accident is most often associated with personal harm or injury. For the sake of simplicity, an accident will be defined here in the broadest possible way to include happenings that have a significant adverse effect on, for example, the constancy of services or the development of an information system, as in the context of

1

DOI: 10.4324/9781003083115-1

the National Programme for Information Technology (NPfIT) project (see the textbox below).

Although near-misses amount to valuable warnings about the bad things that could happen (see Figure 1.1), but carry little risk of jeopardising reliable performance, we tend to fixate on high-impact accidents and how to contain them in a resilient manner. This is not surprising as we are more attracted and powerfully motivated by high-probability, high-impact events (see Chapter 4), which we can heroically contain. Those of us who do contain and limit the consequences of an accident become acclaimed champions in organisations; those who manage to prevent an accident end up as unsung heroes.

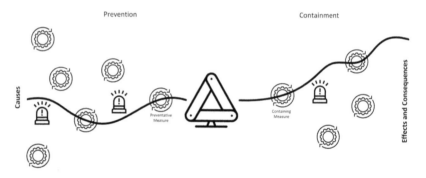

Figure 1.1 Bow-tie.

And yet, although less compelling, devoting attention and effort to near-misses pays off in the long run. Often referred to as the strategy of small losses (Sitkin, 1992), we should highlight near-misses that presage accidents, crises, and disasters:

> Opportunities for learning from near misses are not only less costly and less threatening than learning from larger failures, but they are also much more numerous. Estimates suggest that between several hundred to several thousand near misses occur in an organisation for each major accident.

(Madsen, 2018, p. 155)

To be truly proactive and opportunistic, to prevent near-miss incidents from turning into accidents, and in turn, into a crisis, we should begin by embracing the challenges of not having sufficient historical data to anticipate accidents, let alone near-miss incidents, with confidence. Hence, every impending incident may involve a degree of uncertainty and ambiguity that strips us of the capability of predicting near-misses with accuracy and thereby preventing potential accidents from snowballing into a crisis. Nevertheless, a reliable, mindful approach to managing both near-miss incidents and accidents provides us with an invaluable opportunity to avert adversity that could escalate into a crisis, and subsequently into an irrecoverable disaster if left untreated.

The National Programme for Information Technology – suffering paradox

The UK National Health Service (NHS) is a health care system funded and treasured by the public in the United Kingdom. Perceived to be the envy of the world, it provides free health services such as personal health care.

In 2002, the NPfIT (subsequently re-christened Connecting for Health) was launched. With an original budget of £6.2 billion, it constituted the largest public sector information technology programme ever attempted in the United Kingdom. At the core of this programme was the intention of launching the NHS into the twenty-first century, by implementing an integrated, electronic patient record system that was supposed to replace an ageing analogue filing architecture.

From the outset, this programme ran into trouble. Driven by an overly ambitious political agenda to pursue an unwieldy centralised model of top-down decisions on behalf of local organisations, the programme was plagued by delays, cost overruns, and deteriorating relationships between programme stakeholders. Ultimately, in 2011, the largest ever public sector project was dismantled with costs incurred in excess of £10 billion.

This example of a disastrous endeavour may sound familiar to you. In hindsight, we tend to be puzzled about our inability to remain resilient in the face of unexpected problems and issues that derail our well-thought-out plans. So what is it that we do? We wed ourselves to a just-this-way management of adversity, gravitating to one pole with our entrenched monolithic thinking.

NPfIT – just-this-way

In the case of the NPfIT project, the core definition of how to operate in this project was defined by a single pole: compliance (see Figure 1.2). A detailed plan was devised and broken down into its parts. Managers were expected to become compliant, strictly following a rule book that was informed by major project management frameworks. As a result, the project started to operate on autopilot, with the plan symbolising a rigid direction and managers mindlessly sticking with an inflexible set of actions.

3

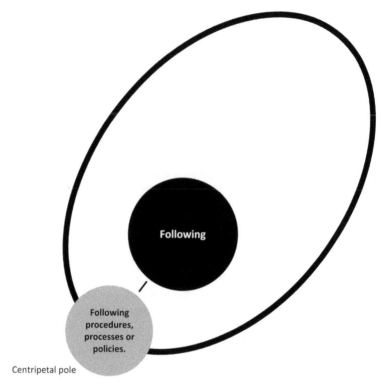

Centripetal pole

Figure 1.2 Just-this-way (following).

NPfIT – just-for-now

Over time, however, performance deteriorated as was indicated by milestones being missed and releases of software versions plagued by system crashes and lack of usability. As the situation began to resemble a crisis, managers abandoned the notion of strict compliance. Just-for-now (see Figure 1.3), managers gravitated to the opposite pole. The notion of doing something different, thinking outside the box (in this case, the rulebook), became the norm. Why not? In the face of unreliable performance, it was evident that following procedures, processes, or policies had not worked.

Unfortunately, although the project embraced the opposite pole of not responding at all, delaying or innovating a response, that was not sustainable for long, as the extent of the flexibility generated by the just-for-now pole did not keep pace with the provision of resources necessary to enable the ignoring, delaying, or innovation of responses. In short, people were empowered to be non-compliant and yet could not exploit the new freedoms because they were still hampered by budget constraints and a culture defined by the notion of compliance.

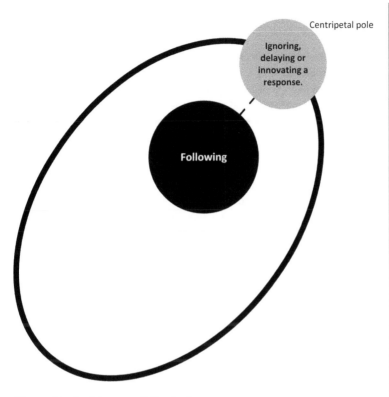

Figure 1.3 Just-for-now (following).

The NHS programme epitomises our paradoxical struggle to manage adversity by relying on 'either' just-this-way 'or' just-for-now thinking. The conventional, and often espoused as self-evidently correct, just-this-way of organisational functioning is defined by consistency in action. The logic of this way of working posits that performance can be achieved through following a prescribed repertoire of decision-making rules and their associated actions (Butler and Gray, 2006). A rule-based response is understood to be an attempt to make the best 'automated' choice from many of those past-informed choices, reducing situated cognition as a source of error. Hence, over the years, organisations have deeply embedded rule-based behaviours in their culture. Deviations from governance, risk, and governance frameworks are discouraged; consistency in action is incentivised and rewarded.

However, therein lies the paradox (Reason, 2008). The restriction and suppression of situated human cognition through a regime of strict compliance undermine organisational capability to deal with the unexpected. In other words, a workforce that runs on autopilot is unable to deal with the unexpected unless it switches it off and replaces its habitual and pre-configured actions with mindful real-time creation of rules, processes, and routines that match the novelty of the situation at hand.

In this respect, the outcome of the NPfIT was down to the fallibility of us human beings. From its inception, a range of near-miss incidents went unheeded. People's mental risk registers were not set up to pick up warning signals they had not experienced in the past. To make matters worse, once those signals were noticed, they were simplified (see Chapter 4) to such an extent that they did not require any further attention. Once near-misses turned into incidents with potentially significant consequences, the project team was not able to switch off that project-wide autopilot mentality (epitomising just-this-way) that people had become so accustomed to. Not surprisingly, they could not deliver reliable performance at any point in time, as they kept on pivoting between two extreme ways of working.

Reliable performance through mindful organising

Preventing near-misses and accidents from spiralling into disasters has been the subject of a range of literature, including the literature on high-reliability organisations (HROs). The last 25 years have seen an abundance of research into HROs that operate in high-hazard environments but have far fewer incidents than one would expect, given the highly hazardous context in which they operate (Rochlin, 1996). These HROs rarely suffer a catastrophic failure in their operations (LaPorte and Consolini, 1991).

What these organisations have in common has been outlined by Rochlin (1993):

1. The organisation is required to maintain high levels of operational reliability and/or safety if it is to be allowed to continue to carry out its tasks (LaPorte and Consolini, 1991).
2. The organisation is also required to maintain high levels of capability, performance, and service to meet public and/or economic expectations and requirements (Roberts, 1990a, 1990b).
3. Because of the consequences of error and failure, the organisation cannot easily make marginal trade-offs between capacity and safety. In the deepest sense, safety is not negotiable (Paul Schulman, 1993).
4. As a result, the organisation is reluctant to allow primary task-related learning to proceed by the usual modalities of trial and error for fear that the first error will be the last trial (LaPorte and Consolini, 1991).
5. Because of the complexity of both technology and task environment, the organisation must actively manage its activities and technologies in real-time while maintaining capacity and flexibility to respond to events and circumstances that can at most be generally bounded (Roberts, 1990a, 1990b).

6. The organisation will be judged to have 'failed' – either operationally or socially – if it does not perform at high levels. Whether it is service or safety that is degraded, the degradation will be noticed and condemned almost immediately (Rochlin, La Porte, and Roberts, 1998).

To summarise, HROs

> have a big incentive to contain the unexpected because when they fail to do so, the results can be catastrophic. Lives can be lost, but so can assets, careers, reputations, legitimacy, credibility, support, trust and goodwill.

(Weick and Sutcliffe, 2001, p. 18)

More recently, research into HROs has concentrated on more ordinary, low-hazard environments that also present a need for reliable performance, such as information systems projects (Denyer *et al.*, 2011; Kutsch, Browning, and Hall, 2014), healthcare (Vogus and Sutcliffe, 2011), train operations (Jeffcott *et al.*, 2006), railways (Busby, 2006), electricity provision (Roe and Schulman, 2008), and banking (Roberts and Libuser, 1993).

This discrete body of research acknowledges that in a complex world, not all failure can be prevented, but impending adversity - signalled by near-misses, a failure of reliable performance on its own (Weick and Sutcliffe 2015) - can be anticipated and, if it is transmuted into accidents, it can be contained. As a pivotal milestone in the development of this literature, Weick and Sutcliffe (2007) codified the HRO concept as one of an attentional state of mindfulness (Weick and Sutcliffe, 2006, 2015), defined as

> The combination of ongoing scrutiny of existing expectations, continuous refinement and differentiation of expectations based on newer experiences, willingness and capability to invent new expectations that make sense of the unprecedented events, a more nuanced appreciation of context and ways to deal with it, and identification of new dimensions of context that improve foresight and current functioning.

(Weick and Sutcliffe, 2001, 32)

Five organisational principles have been established as reliability-enhancing, namely: preoccupation with failure; reluctance to simplify; sensitivity to operations; deference to expertise; and commitment to resilience.

1. Preoccupation with failure is characterised by a *"chronic unease"* (Reason, 2008) regarding small errors that may be a sign of more significant problems. HROs are encouraged to look out openly and transparently for weak signals of impending adversity (Weick and Roberts, 1993).

7

2. Reluctance to simplify is based on the idea that simple cause-effect logic is unwarranted in a complex situation and that a more profound understanding is necessary to comprehend the issues. Multiple, cross-functional viewpoints can help to gain a greater understanding and avoid a single (potentially limited) perspective.

3. Sensitivity to operations refers to an organisational emphasis on big-picture awareness of ongoing work, together with an understanding of how any perturbations may affect other aspects of the organisation. This needs a commitment to drawing on staff's understanding of the impact of their work on others and taking necessary steps to share information freely with minimal bureaucratic barriers.

4. Deference to expertise means that, when necessary, hierarchically senior staff will defer to the domain-specific knowledge and judgement of those closest to the incident (e.g. an engineer with proficiency in a particular issue or with a critical piece of equipment).

5. Finally, commitment to resilience implies that the organisation can bounce back from issues quickly, responding rapidly, and improvising where necessary. This relies on training, investment in key skills, preparation and trust development before incidents occur.

None of these five concepts of a collective mind is easy to establish, let alone to maintain; each depends on an organisational culture that is hard to build but easy to discourage. Rushing to inappropriate solutions, overriding knowledgeable staff, or blaming the bringer of unwelcome news could rapidly unravel HRO principles.

Exploring paradoxes

By now, you may have realised that high-reliability management is not a question of either/or. In the context of the NPfIT project, overusing the just-this-way of mere compliance did not work, nor was the opposite extreme of abandoning the rule book, even if just-for-now, sustainable. In both cases, reliable performance was not established:

> … it is impossible to write procedures to anticipate all situations and conditions that shape people's work (Hirschborn 1993; Sutcliffe 2011). Even if it were possible to craft procedures for every situation, too many rules can create unwanted and even harmful complexity (Katz-Navon, Naveh and Stern, 2005). People can lose flexibility in the face of too many rules and procedures. In some instances compliance with detailed operating procedures is critical in achieving reliability, in part because it creates operational

discipline. But blind adherence is unwise if it reduces the ability to adapt or to react swiftly to unexpected surprises (Sutcliffe 2011). The idea that standard operating procedures and invariant routines are means through which reliable outcomes occur, conflates variation and stability and makes it more difficult to understand the mechanism of reliable performance under dynamic, varying conditions (Weick, Sutcliffe, and Obstfeld 1999; Weick and Sutcliffe 2006; Levinthal and Rerup 2006).

(Sutcliffe, 2018, p. 65)

So, it appears that HROs are not characterised by monolithic, either just-this-way or just-for-now thinking. Instead, HROs

... seek an ideal of perfection but never expect to achieve it. They demand complete safety but never expect it. They dread surprise but always antici-pate it. They deliver reliability but never take it for granted. They live by the book but are unwilling to die by it. If these beliefs seem wonderfully contradictory, those who express them are under no particular pressure to rationalise their paradoxes, indeed, they seem actively to resist such ration-alisation. This lack of goal rationalisation extends to the organisational as well as the individual level. The observed deliberate, and often self-conscious, effort to create and maintain multiple modes of decision making and duplicative error searching regimes, and to hold differing perspectives and rank-ordering of preferences by different groups is a manifestation of collective organisational response rather than individual behavior. Such representational ambiguity is implicitly (and sometimes explicitly) acknowledged and accepted by the organisation, not just as part of the cost of maintaining performance levels, but as an active contributor to problem solving.

(Rochlin, 1993, p. 24)

Basically, the effectiveness of an HRO is due to its ability to manage paradoxes in its approach to the anticipation and containment of near-miss incidents and accidents. The term paradox originates from the Greek *paradoxos*, combining the words *para* (beyond) and *dokein* (to think). A paradox means to ponder beyond the established limits of our thinking, allowing ourselves to be chal-lenged by the presence of simultaneous contradictions, which may appear as mixed messages, conflicting demands, or opposing perspectives (Schad *et al.*, 2016). Paradoxical thinking entails considering 'both/and', and pulling together the opposing demands individuals face, thereby offering an important *"princi-ple [for] dealing with individual cognitions that engage paradox"* (Schad *et al.*, 2016, p. 41).

The study

The abundance of research into HROs has undoubtedly advanced our understanding of what constitutes the high-reliability management of near-misses and accidents:

> The HRO research perspective has its own conceptual and empiri-cal difficulties. The research has centred on a small number of selective case studies at a single slice in time for each organisa-tion. These few cases do not constitute a proven argument that the features identified in the organisations were truly necessary ones (Schulman, 1993). Further, high-reliability organisations research in some respects asserted high reliability as a defining characteristic rather than a performance variable of its organisations. This leaves unanswered the question of which features, if any, and in what amounts or combinations, can contribute to higher reliability (along a continuum) in organisations. Fortunately, more recent research has begun to broaden the analytic focus on reliability from structure to process in organisations, especially the cognitive and sense-making skills and strategies of their members (Weick, Sutcliffe, and Obstfeld 1999; Sanne 1999; Weick and Sutcliffe 2001; see also Hodgkinson and Sparrow 2002).
>
> (Roe and Schulman, 2008, p. 58)

Despite these achievements, much of the research on HROs looks at the management of adversity from a rather monolithic, either/or perspec-tive. For example, the research looking into managerial processes tends to be labelled as either mindful or mindless, based on a perspective of research done in hindsight. In the absence of failure, managerial action is concluded to be mindful; materialising adversity is associated with mind-less behaviour.

So far, much of the research appears to fuel an increasingly polarised debate about what constitutes high-reliability management and whatever else. From a practitioner's perspective, the black/white distinction may well foster greater discrimination between mindfulness and mindlessness, amplifying a constant swing of the pendulum between extreme just-this-way and just-for-now thinking.

However, as already indicated above, the notion of the effectiveness of an HRO is dependent on balancing tensions between simultaneous opposites. Consequently, this book draws on an integrative, as opposed to discrimina-tory, paradox lens on both/and, just-in-case and just-in-time thinking. This perspective is not new. Paradox theory has progressed our comprehension of simultaneous opposites in the context of organisational change (Quinn and Cameron, 1988), leadership (Lewis, Andriopoulos, and Smith, 2014), and learning (Lewis and Dehler, 2000). Adopting a paradox lens for this book, a group of Cranfield University researchers carried out a study to unpack the belief systems of managers regarding their approach to producing reliable performance in the face of adversity; we wanted to explore the process orientation of managers (Roe and Schulman, 2008) anticipating and responding to near-misses and accidents, focusing on the following research question:

How do managers construe the simultaneous opposites of anticipating and responding to near-misses and accidents?

To further conceptualise this research question (see Figure 1.4), in light of recent debates in the paradox literature, the concept of a construct as the conceptual core with centripetal and centrifugal poles buffering its boundaries (Schad, Lewis, and Smith, 2019) is used.

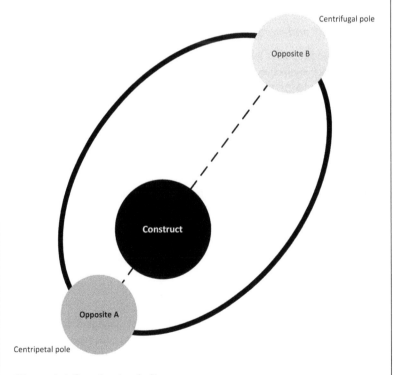

Figure 1.4 Construct polarity.

Construct

Exploring the paradoxical logic of an HRO requires a different epistemology that corresponds well with the performative definition of managers who *"develop their own tentative models"* (Kelly, 1955, 1991) of simultaneous opposites: constructive alternativism. A construct that individuals rely on to give meaning to their lived experiences is bipolar: *"A construct is a way in which some things are construed as being alike and yet different from others"* (Kelly, 1955, p. 74).

In adopting a constructivist epistemology, we argue that high-reliability professionals continuously (re)construe their reality as they *"develop their own tentative models or personal theories about the world in order to understand and negotiate their environments"* (Zuber-Skerritt and Roche, 2004). We posit that the experience of the world around us is open to a plethora of interpretations. Hence, no single construct is final, nor does it ultimately explain the world; instead, it is open to ongoing revision that allows us to continuously comprehend and navigate the world through anticipation. In turn, these revised constructs are being put to the test, determining our feelings, thoughts, and behaviours.

Centripetal and centrifugal poles

It has been proposed that constructs have opposing polar characteristics and that our subjective meaning-making is aided by such bipolarity (e.g. Kelly, 1955, 1970, 1991). For example, the concept of 'good' becomes meaningful if compared and contrasted with 'bad' or similar opposites. In this study, the epistemology of constructive alternativism allows for the creative and diverse interpretations of our world in ways that make better sense to us personally by relying on our mental models that are characterised by opposite poles.

To capture the extent to which a manager gravitates to one pole or the other, we distinguish between centripetal and centrifugal poles. The centripetal pole defines the core characterisation of a managerial process, while the centrifugal pole spans and expands its boundaries (Schad, Lewis, and Smith, 2019).

Repertory grid interview technique

To uncover the personal, deep-seated systems of managers' bipolar constructs in relation to how they construe anticipation of and response to near-misses and accidents, we applied a repertory grid interview technique. The repertory grid is an instrument designed to capture the dimensions and structure of personal meaning. Its aim is to describe the ways in which people give meaning to their experiences in their own terms. It is not so much a test in the conventional sense of the word as a structured interview designed to make those constructs with which persons organise their world more explicit. The way in which we get to know and interpret our milieu, our understanding of ourselves and others is guided by an implicit theory which is the result of conclusions drawn from our experiences. In its many forms, the repertory grid is a method used to explore the structure and content of these implicit theories/personal meanings through which we perceive and act in our day-to-day existence.

In comparison with other research methods, an advantage of the repertory grid technique is, first, the articulation of an interviewee's 'world' in accordance with their personal constructs. As Dick and Jankowicz (2001, p. 187) stated:

> There are a number of advantages to using repertory grid. First, it is a method that avoids the use of a priori categories, but since research participants are asked to construe the same phenomena (i.e. effective performance) it is nevertheless systematic enough to allow the identification of shared cognitions. Second, the technique allows participants to articulate their experiences in their own words, yet, due to its systematic nature, enables the researcher to probe participants' responses such that they are rendered intelligible. Finally, the data obtained from repertory grids is both rich enough to enable a thorough examination of the content of each individual's construct system, yet sufficiently parsimonious to allow rigorous content analysis that can be checked for reliability.

In addition, the use of the repertory grid interview technique provides a non-invasive (Jankowicz, 2004) method that reduces interviewer bias while enabling the interviewer to elicit tacit knowledge of paradoxical tensions.

Context and sample

The 'personal scientists' (Kelly, 1955) in this study are project managers who daily anticipate and respond to near-misses and accidents in the context of complex military procurement projects. Such project managers embody interpretive, experience-based work, and thus represent the desired level of responsibility for analysis. The environment of a project differs from the contexts of the original HRO studies in two important ways. First, in some of these contexts cost of failure is grave but not necessarily life-threatening. Second, managers often do not have command and control over the organisation's technical core (Roberts, 2009). However, these environments also suffer from adverse events that are *"physical, cultural, and emotional event[s] incurring social loss"* (Vaughan, 2016, p. 292). The failure of military procurement projects has the potential for significant disruption, data loss, damage to reputation and may even jeopardise long-term business survival. Failures of such projects have caught public and media attention (e.g. National Audit Office, 2016), have been widespread and have occurred in the private, public and voluntary sectors and in many industries. While research has focused on major incidents, other 'ordinary', low hazard environments such as military procurement projects frequently occur beyond the gaze of research.

The selection of project managers to be respondents was purposeful. First, the individuals singled out had the greatest exposure and in-depth knowledge about near-misses and accidents. Second, they were equipped with extensive authority and responsibility to enact an organisational response to a near-miss or accident. Overall, we carried out 103 repertory grid interviews with managers involved in military procurement projects.

Data elicitation

The elicited components of a repertory grid interview are Elements, Constructs and Ratings.

Elements

These are real-life incidents that illustrate the topic of anticipating and responding to adversity. In accordance with a repertory grid protocol, the interviewees – managers in military procurement projects – were asked to identify three recently experienced and managed near-misses and three accidents, defined as:

- Near-miss incident: unplanned event that has the potential to cause, but does not actually result in human injury, environmental or equipment damage, an interruption to normal operation, or the failure to meet project and programme objectives.

- Accident: unplanned event that results in human injury, environmental or equipment damage, an interruption to normal operation, or the failure to meet project and programme objectives.

Constructs

This is the most important component of the repertory grid; it is where the elements are compared with one another to produce a series of statements that describe what the interviewee thinks about the anticipation and response to near-misses and accidents. These statements formed the eventual unit of analysis. They are bipolar. In other words, every statement is presented as an opposing end of a pole.

Out of the six elements of near-misses and accidents, the interviewees were given three (out of the six) elements in line with a predefined rotation (shown in Table 1.1 by an asterisk). Then, the following central question was asked:

Considering these three incidents, please think about how two of these were similar, and thereby different from the third one, in regard to how you and your team anticipated these incidents and responded to them?

A laddering question (Jankowicz, 2004) *"What does the [construct] mean to you in regards to anticipating and responding to this incident"* was applied to elicit more detail about the expressed construct.

Table 1.1 An Example of a RepGrid (Interviewee 5)

Construct (Score 1)		a	b	c	d	e	f		Construct POLE (Score 5)
		*		*		*			
Not following process or planned mitigations	1	1	3	3	5	2	4	1	Followed process or planned mitigations
		*		*			*		
Unique innovative response	2	5	2	4	5	3	1	2	Boiler plate process followed in response
		*			*	*			
Hard skills response	3	2	3	3	1	5	4	3	Soft skills response
		*			*	*			
Weak leadership	4	2	3	3	1	5	4	4	Strong leadership
			*	*		*			
Single group working	5	2	2	3	3	4	5	5	Multi cross-organisational working
			*	*			*		
Individual	6	1.5	1	3	4.5	5	4	6	Team

* indicates the selection of element cards.

Ratings

This step of clarification of relevance of constructs to the respondent followed the definition of two extreme poles. For example, if the construct chosen by the interviewee was *"experience"*, the interviewee was then asked: *"How would you define the two extremes of experience"?* According to their definitions of the construct poles, the interviewees were then asked to rate all six of their elements on a scale of 1 to 5.

The process of providing the respondents with a different set of three elements was repeated up to eight times or stopped at a stage when an interviewee struggled to identify any further personal constructs. The supplied outcome constructs, to be related (on the same scale of 1–5) by the interviewee in iteration 9 to 10 were as follows:

1. Late Anticipation (Rating 1) versus Early Anticipation (Rating 5)
2. Late Activation of Response (Rating 1) versus Early Activation of Response (Rating 5)

With 103 repertory grids, we arrived at a dataset that included 618 elements, of which 309 constituted an accident and 309 were near-miss incidents. Overall, 659 constructs were extracted, yielding an average of 6.4 constructs per repertory grid interview.

Data aggregation

In order to evaluate qualitative differences between the extracted constructs, a core categorisation procedure was followed (Jankowicz, 2004). Two groups of two researchers were provided with construct cards. These construct cards included the interviewee's definition of the construct and construct pole, as well as an informing quote. In a manual process, the two groups of researchers compared each construct and defined construct categories (see Table 1.2).

The resulting construct categories were checked for reliability in an iterative manner. In a second step, to facilitate the process of identifying similarities and differences between two sets of construct categories, frequency queries of the interviewees' construct and construct definitions were created. In a 'reliability workshop', the two groups of researchers compared and contrasted each derived NVivo word cloud to produce (dis)agreement of construct categories. For the final stage of the coding and reliability process, a fifth researcher (researcher E) received the resulting reliability table, word clouds and all the construct cards. The final step of the check and validation process resulted in reducing the number of construct categories to 14, with a reliability index of 76%.

Table 1.2 Coding and Reliability Process

Measure	Coding/Reliability Process		
	Initial Coding	**Recalibration**	**Validation**
Process	Initial Categorisation	Word clouds Enhanced categorisation	Reliability Table Word Clouds Construct Cards Pareto Analysis
Number of categories	Team 1 (A&B): 24 Team 2 (C&D): 18	Team 1 (A&B): 18 Team 2 (C&D): 17	Independent Researcher E
Agreed common constructs	23	18	14
Inter-code reliability	56%	68%	76%

Determination of salient construct categories

The elicitation of common constructs was further determined by relying on the analysis of Unique Frequency (UF). Common constructs were identified as 'salient' if they were mentioned by at least 25% of the interviewees (Lemke, Goffin, and Szwejczewski, 2003; Goffin, Lemke, and Szwejczewski, 2006; Goffin and Koners, 2011; Lemke, Clark, and Wilson, 2011; Raja *et al.*, 2013).

Analysis of centripetal and centrifugal poles

In the late 1970s, Peter Honey, an occupational psychologist, developed a technique that allowed the analysis of multiple grid data. He pre-supplied a construct that was relevant to the investigation of the grid data and measured the 'distance' of the ratings for each elicited construct from the supplied construct. Such a measurement of 'distance' helped in identifying which elicited personal constructs were closest to the supplied construct.

The high-reliability professional as a paradox navigator

Within the confines of a dual yet dynamic, intricate, and paradoxical world of high-reliability management, we as high-reliability professionals navigate our lived learning experiences to engage with an ongoing process of coping with (Handy, 1994; Simons, 1999) or working through (Lüscher and Lewis, 2008) the competing demands of polarities and their associated tensions. There is hope, though:

> The managers of high reliability organisations begin with a clear specifica-
> tion of core events that simply must not happen (Laporte, 1996). To this
> they add the specifications, through careful examination of experience and
> causal analysis, of a set of precursor events [near misses] or conditions that
> could lead to core events that pose unacceptable hazards to the organisation
> and beyond. The precluded and precursor events bound an "envelope" of
> reliability within which these organisations seek to operate.
>
> HROs develop elaborate procedures to constrain behaviour and task per-
> formance within the envelope. At the same time, the organisations feature
> a "culture of reliability" that is widespread, shared mindfulness of condi-
> tions that might causally lead to error and failure (Langer, 1989; Weick and
> Roberts, 1993).
>
> (Roe and Schulman, 2008, pp. 54–55)

Although establishing and sustaining a culture of mindfulness is covered in more detail in Chapter 11, we need further advice on what the *"elaborate procedures to constrain behaviour"* means. It should not signify a customary or unchanging and often mechanically performed monolithic process or procedure, a just-this-way activity of anticipating and responding to near misses and accidents. That would be mindless!

Instead, a high-reliability manager *"continually builds, elaborates, and tests"* (Clarke, 1986, p. 335) their hardwired construction of polarities around the management of adversity. This process of reconstruction and reconfiguration requires *"methodological support"* (Pavlovic and Stojnov, 2020, p. 323) as a means to provide a *"temporary resolution of the inherent paradoxes of their lived experiences"* (Wright, 2020, p. 307), as displayed in Figure 1.5.

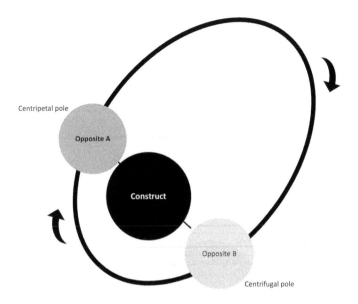

Figure 1.5 Reconstruction and reconfiguration.

The following textbox provides a glimpse into how we could and should approach paradoxical tensions as high-reliability managers. Moving beyond mindless just-this-way and just-for-now, we need to set the scene for mindful just-in-case thinking, to be practised in real-time, just-in-time.

The National Programme for Information Technology – navigating paradox

To recap, in the context of the NPfIT project, the predominant just-this-way mode of managing adversity was a somewhat slavish adherence to follow-ing rules and procedures. This may not be surprising given that the notion of compliance, with little freedom to mindfully deviate from project manage-ment frameworks, is a given in civil service projects.

The materialisation of adversity essentially swung the pendulum the other way, so that the rulebook was largely suspended, just-for-now, as novel solu-tions were needed quickly. However, this opposing operating mode was not sustainable, so the project tumbled into a crisis from which it did not recover.

NPfIT – just-in-case
With the benefit of hindsight, it is easy to say that the project should have embraced a both/and mentality to allow project members to both

19

follow procedures, processes, or policies and ignore, delay, or innovate a response if deemed necessary, just-in-case (see Figure 1.6).

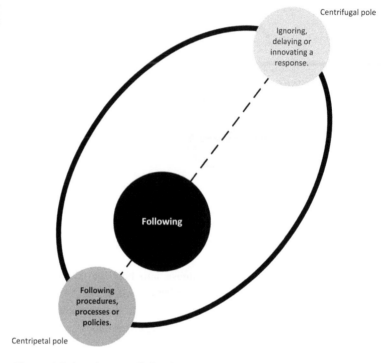

Figure 1.6 Just-in-case (following).

So why is it so difficult to embrace both poles (as indicated in Figure 1.6) with a preference for a centripetal pole but still leaving the door open to have a bit of both centripetal and centrifugal wisdom to define our core approach to managing adversity?

> As attractive and important as it might be to embrace polarities and hold a both/and mindset, it is an endeavour easier said than done. The task is harder than we might like because, to some degree, the decks are stacked against us. Our hardwiring, our language, and the evolving way we make sense of the world all seem to conspire against our best efforts to see the world with a both/and mindset.
>
> (Emerson and Lewis, 2019, p. 15)

Our evolution as human beings, the development of our egos, is character-ised by either/or, black/white, and right/wrong thinking. In many cases, our sensemaking of the world is truly either/or:

- Either I am alive or I am dead

- Either I will buy that product or I will save the money

- Either I am a risk-taking or a risk-averse person

- Either this equation is right or it is wrong

These clear-cut either/or distinctions are trained into us, be it in school or in our professional lives:

> The threat to our ego can trigger responses in the brain that drive people to protect themselves and, in turn, lower their willingness to be open and vulnerable to other ways of seeing and being.
>
> (Emerson and Lewis, 2019, p. 21)

We take sides in a polarised world, protecting our egos. Despite (or because of) our experience, when was the last time we blurted out or heard some-body else say:

- Of course, this is the right answer!

- Naturally, this is what we have to do!

- I know what to do!

- There is only one side to this!

Our side on the either/or spectrum has already been picked; most likely, we overemphasise and overuse one pole while questioning the existence of an opposite alternative. Why? Because, when considering the 'other' pole in isolation, it may sound absurd, unfamiliar, and not normal. Also, it is more convenient to jump to conclusions without making an effort to integrate both centripetal and centrifugal poles.

So, let's make an effort and embrace a both/and mindset by making osten-sible contradictions co-exist simultaneously in the form of a third way:

> The Third Alternative isn't my way, it isn't your way – it's our way. It's not a compromise between your way and my way; it's better than a compromise. A third alternative is what the Buddhists call the other two ways, like the tip of a triangle.
>
> The Third Alternative is a better alternative than any that have been proposed. It is a product of sheer creative effort.
>
> (Covey, 2013, p. 187)

21

Coming back to the NPfIT case study, the project members, as a foundation of high-reliability management, should have expended greater effort on exploring this third, just-in-case, way concerning the construct of the 'Following' (see Figure 1.3) to define third-way working principles

- that combine the benefits and balance the adverse ramifications of both centripetal and centrifugal poles;

- that challenge dogmatic thinking; and

- that widen their response repertoire.

Sadly, as in the NPfIT case study, such effort is scarce in modern-day organising that is circumscribed by mindless, polarised, dogmatic, and routine-based reliability, put forward as self-evidently correct.

NPfIT – just-in-time

It is easy to suggest that in the NPfIT project, project members should have made a genuine effort to engage with just-in-case both/and thinking, but they did not for the reasons already mentioned. In other words, it would have been unwise to set in stone a possible third both/and configuration of polarity, as it would challenge the stability and certainty of clear-cut either/or just-this-way thinking.

The ultimate challenge of paradoxical thinking is to continually reconfigure centripetal and centrifugal forces, in real-time, according to the contextual conditions we face (see Figure 1.7). A third way that allows us to integrate the forces of both the centripetal and centrifugal poles would be in constant flux. This could imply that a centrifugal force – just-in-time – can become the centripetal authority commanding the core definition of the third both/and way of managing adversity in a highly reliable manner.

The trajectory of the NPfIT is a typical example that is often given of the contributory factors to a crisis or disaster: our extreme pivoting from a just-this-way to a just-for-now pole:

> When this happens, the system gets stuck and a vicious cycle can begin in which groups become entrenched, lose momentum, and make no progress. In addition, there are ripple effects created that extend well beyond the issue at hand and wreak havoc in ways that have nothing to do with the polarity being encountered.
>
> (Emerson and Lewis, 2019, p. 21)

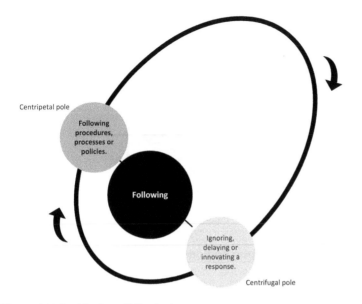

Centripetal pole

Following
procedures,
processes or
policies.

Following

Ignoring,
delaying or
innovating a
response.

Centrifugal pole

Figure 1.7 Just-in-time (following).

Breaking such a vicious cycle in the NPfIT project would have demanded effortful, arduous, and trying paradoxical just-in-case and just-in-time thinking. By embracing simultaneous opposites, a key characteristic of effective HROs, we become mindful of alternative options in performing reliably, undeterred by adversity.

Navigating paradoxes

Throughout our professional life, we develop opinions, beliefs, habits, and routines, often dogmatically, that tell us the one best way of anticipating and responding to actual and near-miss incidents. Our way of working becomes self-evidently correct, reinforced by biases that not only inhibit our impartial judgement but also reinforce monolithic just-this-way thinking.

In this respect, this book is not supposed to be another just-this-way guide that prescribes what is right or wrong. It does not provide another immovable view of how to achieve high-reliability performance. Instead, it takes you on a journey of exploration using rudimentary navigation, relying on a map and a compass.

Step 1: Choosing a good map

A map (see Figure 1.8) is the most important and invaluable aid. It shows you the terrain that you need to cover. As a high-reliability professional, it may tell you what

23

adversity you could encounter, although never in complete detail; a map does not tell you precisely what weather you will experience or what near-misses and accidents you might meet. Your map may well be a benefits map or a list of critical success factors (see Chapter 2), a detailed risk register or a scenario plan (see Chapter 3).

Figure 1.8 A map.

Step 2: Choosing a good compass

Next to having a map in place you need a compass. The compass needle's red end points to the magnetic north (see Figure 1.9). With the compass we need to manage adversity, our magnetic north indicates the centripetal wisdom that we may dogmatically believe will get us to our destination. Regardless of how we hold our compass, it always points in that direction. Nevertheless, our needle also gives us the opposite to our north.

Figure 1.9 A compass.

Most good compasses allow adjustment for magnetic declination to define the true north. From a just-this-way and just-for-now perspective, you can reset and reconfigure your true north. How true is your just-this-way of management? How beneficial, just-for-now, is the opposite to your true north, the true south on your compass?

Step 3: Taking a bearing on a map

I am not assuming that you read this book because you are an outdoors enthusiast but that you are a high-reliability professional who aims to engage with paradoxical thinking to navigate the world of adversity. Hence, let's assume you

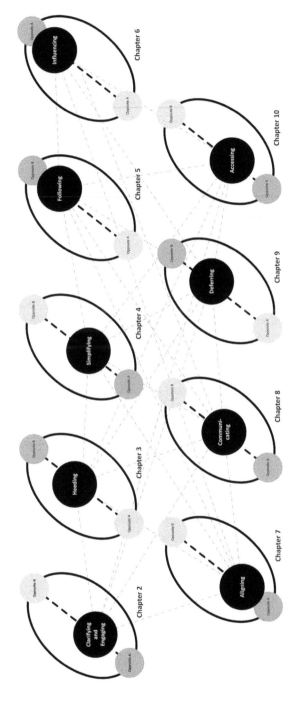

Figure 1.10 Navigating through a construct system of simultaneous bipolar opposites.

do not have a single compass that you place on your map, but nine of them (see Figure 1.10), nine compasses that each represent a bipolar process of managing near-misses and accidents:

- Clarifying and Engaging

- Heeding

- Simplifying

- Following

- Influencing

- Aligning

- Communicating

- Deferring

- Accessing

Each chapter provides you with an additional compass that will introduce you to centripetal wisdom that is grounded in the study we carried out. It will explain why we are tempted by centripetal forces and the biases and inclinations we consider. It then provides the opposite of what we may think of as just-this-way. Just-for-now, you will be confronted by the centripetal pole of managing adversity, one that has turned out to be less preferred, but which is still beneficial. Within the context of the vignette of a case study, we make a case for both/and, just-in-case thinking, attempting to integrate both centripetal and centrifugal forces into a third way for how to anticipate and contain the fallout from near-misses and accidents.

It is possible that just-in-time, paradoxical thinking could leave you with paradox and cognitive overload, resulting in paralysis in decision-making. But that is not what I am aiming for. Instead, I hope that by engaging with simultaneous opposite polarities, any residual dogmatic thinking you have may be challenged and you may come to appreciate the opposite to what you have always considering right; you could create new possibilities for high-reliability management that you have not thought of before.

Have you got your map and compass in front of you? Are you ready to navigate the complex world of adversity? Let's go!

Dr. Elmar Kutsch

References

Busby, J. S. (2006) 'Failure to mobilize in reliability-seeking organizations: Two cases from the UK railway', *Journal of Management Studies*, 43(6), pp. 1375–1393.

Butler, B. S. and Gray, P. H. (2006) 'Reliability, mindfulness, and information systems', *MIS Quarterly*, 30(2), pp. 211–224.

Clarke, C. (1986) 'Ten years of conceptual development in research on teacher thinking', in Ben-Peretz, M., Bromme, R., and Halkes, R. (eds.) *Advances in research on teacher thinking*. Lisse: Swets & Zeitlinger, pp. 7–20.

Covey, S. R. (2013) *The 8th habit: From effectiveness to greatness*. London: Simon & Schuster UK.

Denyer, D. *et al.* (2011) 'Exploring reliability in information systems programmes', *International Journal of Project Management*, 29(4), pp. 442–454.

Dick, P. and Jankowicz, D. (2001) 'A social constructionist account of police culture and its influence on the representation and progression of female officers A repertory grid analysis in a UK police force', *Policing: An International Journal of Police Strategies & Management*, 24(2), pp. 181–199.

Emerson, B. and Lewis, K. (2019) *Navigating polarities: Using both/and thinking to lead transformation*. Washington, DC: Paradoxical Press.

Goffin, K. and Koners, U. (2011) 'Tacit knowledge, lessons learnt, and new product development', *Journal of Product Innovation Management*, 28(2), pp. 300–318.

Goffin, K., Lemke, F. and Szwejczewski, M. (2006) 'An exploratory study of "close" supplier–manufacturer relationships', *Journal of Operations Management*, 24(2), pp. 189–209.

Handy, C. (1994) *The age of paradox*. Boston, MA: Harvard Business School Press.

Hirschbörn, J. (1993) 'Hierarchy versus bureaucracy: The case of a nuclear reactor', in Roberts, K. H. (ed.) *New challenges to understanding organizations*. New York: Macmillan, pp. 137–150.

Hodgkinson, G. P. and Sparrow, P. (2002) *The competent organization: A psychological analysis of the strategic management process*. Buckingham: Open University Press (Managing work and organizations series).

Jankowicz, D. (2004) *The easy guide to repertory grids*. Chichester: John Wiley & Sons, Inc.

Jeffcott, S. *et al.* (2006) 'Risk, trust, and safety culture in U.K. train operating companies', *Risk Analysis*, 26(5), pp. 1105–1121.

Katz-Navon, T. A. L., Naveh, E. and Stern, Z. (2005) 'Safety climate in health care organizations: A multidimensional approach', *Academy of Management Journal*, 48(6), pp. 1075–1089.

Kelly, G. A. (1955) *The psychology of personal constructs*. New York: Norton.

Kelly, G. A. (1970) 'A brief introduction to personal construct theory', in Bannister, D. (ed.) *Perspectives in personal construct theory*. London: Academic Press, pp. 3–20.

Kelly, G. A. (1991) *The psychology of personal constructs*. London: Routledge.

Kutsch, E., Browning, T. R. and Hall, M. (2014) 'Bridging the risk gap: The failure of risk management in information systems projects', *Research Technology Management*, 57(2), pp. 26–32.

Langer, E. (1989) *Mindfulness*. Cambridge: Perseus Publishing.

Laporte, T. R. (1996) 'High reliability organizations: Unlikely, demanding and at risk', *Journal of Contingencies and Crisis Management*, 4(2), pp. 60–71.

LaPorte, T. R. and Consolini, P. M. (1991) 'Working in practice but not in theory', *Journal of Public Administration Research and Theory*, 1(1), pp. 19–48.

Lemke, F., Clark, M. and Wilson, H. (2011) 'Customer experience quality: An exploration in business and consumer contexts using repertory grid technique', *Journal of the Academy of Marketing Science*, 39(6), pp. 846–869.

Lemke, F., Goffin, K. and Szwejczewski, M. (2003) 'Investigating the meaning of supplier-manufacturer relationships – An exploratory study', *International Journal of Physical Distribution and Logistics Management*, 8(1), pp. 12–35.

Levinthal, D. and Rerup, C. (2006) 'Crossing an apparent chasm: Bridging mindful and less-mindful perspectives on organizational learning', *Organization Science*, 17(4), pp. 502–513.

Lewis, M. W. and Dehler, G. E. (2000) 'Learning through paradox: A pedagogical strategy for exploring contradictions and complexity', *Journal of Management Education*, 24(6), pp. 708–725.

Lewis, W., Andriopoulos, C. and Smith, K. W. (2014) 'Paradoxical leadership to enable strategic agility: Torrens University Australia', *California Management Review*, 56(Spring), pp. 58–77.

Lüscher, L. S. and Lewis, M. W. (2008) 'Organizational change and managerial sensemaking: Working through paradox', *Academy of Management Journal*, 51(2), pp. 221–240.

Madsen, P. M. (2018) 'Organizing for reliability: A guide for research and practice', in Ramanujam & K. H. Roberts (eds.), *Organizing for reliability*. Stanford, CA: Stanford University Press, pp. 143–168.

National Audit Office (2016) *Delivering major projects in government: A briefing for the Committee of Public Accounts*. London.

Pavlovic, J. and Stojnov, D. (2020) 'Personal construct coaching', in *The Wiley handbook of personal construct psychology*. Hoboken, NJ: Wiley-Blackwell, pp. 320–329.

Perrow, C. (1999) *Normal accidents: Living with high-risk technologies*. Princeton, NJ: Princeton University Press.

Quinn, R. E. and Cameron, K. S. (1988) *Paradox and transformation: Toward a theory of change in organization and management*. Cambridge, MA: Ballinger Publishing Company.

Raja, J. Z. *et al.* (2013) 'Achieving customer satisfaction through integrated products and services: An exploratory study', *Journal of Product Innovation Management*, 30(6), pp. 1128–1144.

Reason, J. (2008) *The human contribution: Unsafe acts, accidents and heroic recoveries*. Boca Raton: Taylor & Francis.

Roberts, K. H. (1990a) 'Managing high reliability organizations', *California Management Review*, 32(4), pp. 101–113.

Roberts, K. H. (1990b) 'Some characteristics of one type of high reliability organization', *Organization Science*, 1(2), pp. 160–176.

Roberts, K. H. (2009) 'Managing the unexpected: Six years of HRO-literature reviewed', *Journal of Contingencies and Crisis Management*, 17(1), pp. 50–54.

Roberts, K. H. and Libuser, C. (1993) 'From bhopal to banking: Organizational design can mitigate risk', *Organizational Dynamics*, 21(4), pp. 15–26.

Rochlin, G. (1993) 'Defining high reliability organizations in practice: A taxonomic prolegomenon', in Roberts, K. (ed.) *New challenges to understanding organizations*. New York: Macmillan, pp. 11–32.

Rochlin, G. I. (1996) 'Reliable organizations: Present research and future directions', *Journal of Contingencies and Crisis Management*, 4(2), pp. 55–59.

Rochlin, G., La Porte, T. and Roberts, K. (1998) 'The self-designing high-reliability organization: Aircraft carrier flight operations at sea', *Naval War College Review*, 51(3), p. 97.

Roe, E. and Schulman, P. R. (2008) *High reliability management: Operating on the edge*. Stanford, CA: Stanford University Press.

Sanne, J. M. (1999) *Creating safety in air traffic control*. Arkiv (Linköping studies in arts and science). https://www.diva-portal.org/smash/record.jsf?pid=diva2%3A271805&dswid=1217

Schad, J. *et al.* (2016) 'Paradox research in management science: Looking back to move forward', *Academy of Management Annals*, 10(1), pp. 5–64.

Schad, J., Lewis, M. W. and Smith, W. K. (2019) 'Quo vadis, paradox? Centripetal and centrifugal forces in theory development', *Strategic Organization*, 17(1), pp. 107–119.

Schulman, P. R. (1993) 'The analysis of high reliability organizations: A comparative framework', in Roberts, K. H. (ed.) *New challenges to understanding organizations*. New York: Macmillan, pp. 33–54.

Schulman, Paul R. (1993) 'The negotiated order of organizational reliability', *Administration & Society*, 25(3), pp. 353–372.

Simons, P. R. J. (1999) 'Transfer of learning: Paradoxes for learners', *International Journal of Educational Research*, 31(7), pp. 577–589.

Sitkin, S. B. (1992) 'Learning through failure: The strategy of small losses', *Research in Organizational Behavior*, 14, p. 231.

Sutcliffe, K. (2018) 'Mindful organizing', in Ramanujam, R. and Roberts, K. H. (eds.) *Organizing for reliability: A guide for research and practice*. Stanford, CA: Stanford University Press, pp. 61–89.

Sutcliffe, K. M. (2011) 'High reliability organizations (HROs)', *Best Practice & Research Clinical Anaesthesiology*, 25(2), pp. 133–144.

Vaughan, D. (2016) *The challenger launch decision: Risky technology, culture, and deviance at NASA, Enlarged Edition*. Chicago, IL: University of Chicago Press.

Vogus, T. J., and Sutcliffe, K. M. (2007). The impact of safety organizing, trusted leadership, and care pathways on reported medication errors in hospital nursing units. *Medical Care*, 45(10), pp. 997–1002.

Weick, K. and Roberts, K. (1993) 'Collective mind in organizations: Heedful interrelating on flight decks', *Administrative Science Quarterly*, 38(3), p. 357.

Weick, K. and Sutcliffe, K. (2001) *Managing the unexpected: Assuring high performance in an age of complexity*. San Francisco, CA: Jossey Bass.

Weick, K. and Sutcliffe, K. (2006) 'Mindfulness and the quality of organizational attention', *Organization Science*, 17(4), pp. 514–524.

Weick, K. and Sutcliffe, K. (2007) *Managing the unexpected: Resilient performance in an age of uncertainty*. 2nd edn. San Francisco, CA: Jossey Bass.

Weick, K. and Sutcliffe, K. (2015) *Managing the unexpected: Sustained performance in a complex world*. 3rd edn. Hoboken, NJ: Wiley.

Weick, K., Sutcliffe, K. M. and Obstfeld, D. (1999) 'Organizing for high reliability: Processes of collective mindfulness', in Sutton, R. S. and Staw, B. M. (eds.) *Research in organizational behavior*. Stanford, CA: Jai Press, pp. 81–123.

Weick, K. E., Sutcliffe, K. M. and Obstfeld, D. (1999) 'Organizing for high reliability: Processes of collective mindfulness', *Research in Organizational Behavior*, 21, pp. 81–123.

Wright, R. (2020) 'Organizational paradoxes – When opposites cease to be opposites', in Winter, D. and Reed, N. (eds.) *The Wiley handbook of personal construct psychology*. Hoboken, NJ: Wiley-Blackwell.

Zuber-Skerritt, O. and Roche, V. (2004) 'A constructivist model for evaluating postgraduate supervision: A case study', *Quality Assurance in Education*, 12(2), pp. 82–93.

Chapter 2

Clarifying aims, objectives, or outcomes; and engaging with stakeholders

The anticipation and containment of adversity, signified by near-misses and accidents, need to be purposeful and directed towards safeguarding organisational outcomes and outputs that are dear to stakeholders. In this respect, the constructs of both clarifying and engaging are covered in this chapter, as they are, by their very nature, intertwined. Clarifying is about the course or path of thought and action we are taking; achieving clarity in outcomes and objectives requires engaging with multiple stakeholders, and with the resulting uncertainty and ambiguity around the course of action.

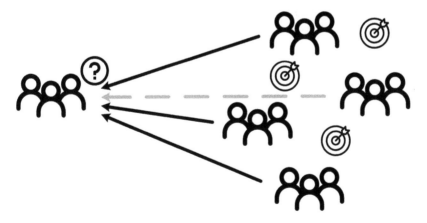

Figure 2.1 Making sense of stakeholder expectations.

The process of clarifying and engaging is constantly challenged. The direction we take may need to be adjusted because stakeholders (see Figure 2.1) change their minds or remain uninterested or invisible. As such, aims, objectives, and

31

DOI: 10.4324/9781003083115-2

outcomes may remain ambiguous; ambiguity sows doubt in us regarding interpretation and clarity around the direction to take:

> … there is the added challenge of complexity and the associated problems
> of imperfect information. Second, additional stakeholders often have dis-
> parate goals, demands and opinions, and they frequently interpret the same
> situation differently.

(Hall and Vredenburg, 2005, p. 13)

In practice (see Figure 2.2), our study has shown that we tend to gravitate towards
a centripetal pole that acknowledges the appreciation of objectives, aims, or outcomes as unclear or not understood (see Chapter 1); in light of such acceptance
of ambiguity, we ignore uninterested or opposed or demotivated stakeholders.

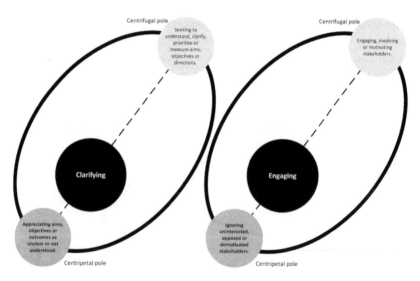

Figure 2.2 Centripetal and centrifugal forces (clarifying and engaging).

Centripetal wisdom

Our preferred core definition of the process of clarifying and engaging is more
influenced by the gravitational forces of the centripetal pole of accepting and
ignoring stakeholder ambiguity. The biases and inclinations enumerated below
pull us towards a core definition of what we end up doing:

Status quo. A preference for maintaining the current state of affairs is referred
to as the *status quo* bias (Samuelson and Zeckhauser, 1988). We are reluctant to

embrace change, whether in decision-making or in how we protect an organisation from adversity.

Ambiguity. The ambiguity effect (Frisch and Baron, 1988) is an inclination to avoid options that we consider incomplete or ambiguous. As we dislike uncertainty, we opt for aims, objectives, and outcomes that we think we know. In essence, we trust what we know and are familiar with.

Anchoring. Subconsciously, we tend to focus on reference points (e.g. a piece of evidence) to make the most informed decision. Usually, the reference point is the first piece of information we receive. This reference is then 'anchored down' with the consequence that we rely on it heavily, regardless of its relevance. This, in turn, will shape our preconceptions of aims, objectives, and outcomes (Kahneman and Lovallo, 2003).

Misrepresentation. Going hand in hand with optimism bias, we tend, at times, to knowingly exaggerate the benefits of a direction desirable to us and other stakeholders (Flyvbjerg, 2008).

Consequently, for the constructs of clarifying and engaging, we are attracted by the idea of stability and clarity (see Figure 2.3). We are inclined to insulate ourselves from the outside world, to be inward-looking, so that stakeholder ambiguity can be downplayed or ignored outright as a nuisance. This centripetal wisdom yields a range of benefits. It provides a sense of stability as we can conserve the status quo; this, in turn, offers clarity in direction. Furthermore, the external environment will not significantly define, shape, and limit our capabilities and skills to prevent the reoccurrence of past-informed incidents.

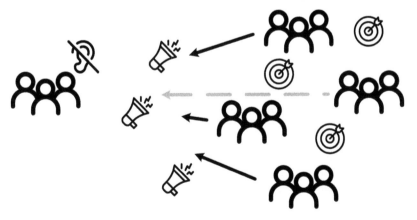

Figure 2.3 Cancelling out stakeholder expectations.

The following toolbox comprises some management methodologies, controls, and techniques that we can draw on to pull us towards supporting centripetal wisdom.

The toolbox

Critical success factors.

> "*The Critical Success Factor methodology is a procedure that attempts to make explicit those few key areas that dictate managerial and organisational success*"
>
> (Boynton and Zmud, 1984, p. 17)

In essence, in line with a top-down structured process (see Figure 2.4), a course of action is directed by the critical internal activities and conditions that allow the organisation to fulfil its mission.

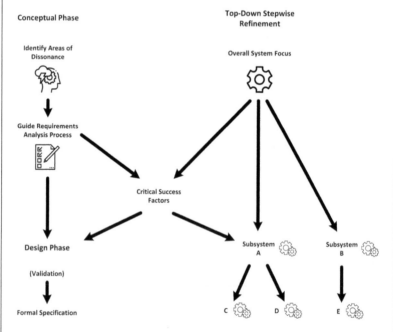

Figure 2.4 The requirements analysis process (Rockart, 1979; adapted from Boynton and Zmud, 1984, p. 21).

Knowing critical success factors can focus our attention on the most beneficial and most needed capabilities that enable better performance management and a realisation of long-term goals and objectives. Resource allocation can be prioritised in accordance with established critical success factors; they can be measured and monitored to ensure a continuous alignment between critical success factors and the organisation's direction.

Disconnection and insulation

By concentrating on what we have been doing and sustaining the course of action we have taken, we may overemphasise our internal skills and capabilities based on what we believe are internal critical success factors. Those, in turn, drive the definition of the direction we take, yet are independent of external stakeholder demands. We thereby insulate and detach ourselves from the outside world.

Preoccupation with success

Being fixated inwards, we may overemphasise past successes, validate the existence of the internal base of skills and capabilities, and resist changing the resource base that served us so well in the past. Why fix something that is not broken?

Reductionism and universality

Once we have anchored a direction (see Anchoring bias), we turn its realisation into manageable entities. In other words, we create a recipe of single success factors that we only have to replicate, regardless of what direction we end up taking. As a consequence, the recipe defines the desired outcome and not vice versa.

Centrifugal wisdom

Centripetal wisdom proclaims an inward-looking, reductionist, view of success factors that is disconnected from stakeholders and fuels the temptation to set a course based on what we have always been good at rather than what we need to do to excel in response to ambiguous stakeholder expectations. This perspective plays well to our inclination to avoid the ambiguity that stems from multiple stakeholder perspectives. So what should we do?

> A recent stream of applied management literature has emphasised the "reach out and touch everyone" approach. For example, Waddock et al. (2002) argued that companies should engage "all stakeholders in continuing dialogue to ensure that the company's values and actions are in accord with society's and stakeholders' expectations." Hart and Sharma (2004) emphasised the business opportunities that lie in recognising and integrating the views of "fringe" stakeholders, defined as those that are disconnected or invisible to the firm because they are remote, weak, poor, disinterested, isolated, nonlegitimate or nonhuman.

35

(Hall and Vredenburg, 2005, p. 13)

In the light of a 'reach out and touch everyone' philosophy, HROs are sensitive and mindful towards stakeholder ambiguity and possible goal conflicts (Roberts, 1990) that may cloud clarity in direction:

> High reliability organisations react to ambiguity by increasing it momentarily. This occurs when they pay more attention to discrepancies, complications, details and ignorance, all in an effort to sustain ongoing projects. To increase ambiguity is to grasp more of the situation. Ambiguity is not about solving puzzles where all the pieces lie on the table awaiting rearrangement. Instead, to 'grasp' ambiguity is to comprehend it adequately, to simplify it self-consciously and to accept that the simplification is fleeting, incomplete and will fail. To grasp ambiguity is to refrain from the simplifications inherent in types, categories, stereotypes and habits. Instead, one settles for a workable level of ambiguity, but no more. To grasp ambiguity is to impose a plausible next step, but then to treat plausibility as both transient and as something compounded of knowledge and ignorance. Grasp is the acceptance that behind ambiguity lies more ambiguity, not clarity. It is the realisation that clarity is costly because it discards so much potential information. And it is the realisation that progress produces complication rather than resolution.
>
> (Weick, 2015, p. 117)

Sensitivity and respect

Sensitivity towards stakeholders constitutes an awareness of their needs and emotions associated with their objectives and outcomes. This implies that we are consulting stakeholders early, often, and face-to-face as a platform on which to establish a personal relationship. By asking questions and challenging assumptions on all sides, these consultations make the tacit understanding of the outcome, objectives, and overall direction explicit (Crilly and Sloan, 2012). Ultimately, stakeholder ambiguity is in the eye of the beholder, so it is up to us to mindfully engage with stakeholder ambiguity respectfully.

Stakeholder participation

Stakeholders are not passive bystanders on whose behalf we are trying to manage looming adversity. Instead, they are value-adding entities who voice their knowledge, experience, perceptions, and ideas. As such, we should bring stakeholders on board to collectively prevent near-miss errors from turning into actual incidents, crises, or disasters. Although stakeholders may not have the principal decision-making power, they may have a say in the final decision.

Bargaining

A lack of clarity in direction, goals, or outcomes may signify a set of diverging priorities. Hence, stakeholders may be prioritised according to their value congruence and the degree to which they offer compatible benefits; they may be valued on the basis of strategic complementarity on the basis of a mutual contribution to each other's strategic needs (see Figure 2.5).

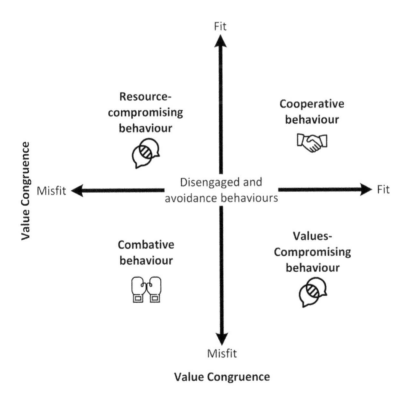

Figure 2.5 An organisation–stakeholder fit framework for relational behaviours (adapted from Bundy, Vogel and Zachary, 2018, p. 491).

37

While we should aim for sufficient consensus on the direction we take, it is not always necessary to aim for absolute consensus, as residual ambiguity fosters creativity and flexibility (Weick, 1979):

> Continuous bargaining over goal priority serves to keep all members of the organisation informed about the activities and needs of all parts of the organisation. Thus, bargaining makes the organisation's "big picture" clear to everyone in the organisation and helps them to coordinate their work (Roberts and Bea, 2001).

(Madsen, 2018, p. 129)

Change in direction

Stakeholder ambiguity may result in the movement of goalposts. As a consequence, we need to be ready to change course at short notice; we may reduce the planning horizon to address continuous stakeholder ambiguity or exploit it as a negotiating currency (Das, 1991).

Adjustment of the resource base

Persistent stakeholder ambiguity does not just imply moving the goalposts; it also implies the constant adjustment of the knowledge, skills, and capabilities base (see Chapters 9 and 10) that we rely on to safeguard the direction we finally decide to take. Moreover, the adjustments to such a resource base require us to alter our processes and routines (see Chapter 6) in a dynamic fashion (Eisenhardt and Martin, 2000), in constant calibration against a stakeholder congruent direction.

Clarity in communication

The role of clarity in direction cannot be overestimated (see Chapter 4), whether it is in verbal or nonverbal form. With all stakeholders involved in active communication, open communication allows stakeholder ambiguity to surface; imbalances between different courses of action need to be allowed to come to light so that we can engage with them positively.

Responsibility and accountability

We may have a preferred direction that we want to pursue to fulfil our objectives and outcomes. We need to communicate about those objectives and outcomes openly, but we also need to own them and be answerable collectively for their realisation.

Trust

The concept of trust has been a reoccurring factor in averting adversity. Trust demonstrates to stakeholders that, despite ambiguity and the resulting fluidity of direction, we are responsible and accountable for doing the "right things". It conveys that we care and commit ourselves to prevent near-misses and accidents from cascading into a crisis that may well affect us all.

Plausibility

To address stakeholder ambiguity, we may aim for greater "*plausibility, pragmatics [and] coherence*" (Weick, 1995, p. 57). Instead of merely aiming for greater accuracy in our assessment of stakeholder ambiguity, we are looking for prioritisation of competing or complementing stakeholder expectations that seem valid or reasonable or intelligible.

Balancing efficiency and reliability

Embracing stakeholder ambiguity is a constant struggle to prioritise and trade-off multiple conflicting objectives or directions. In particular, reliability is under constant threat from our pursuit of short-term efficiencies and profits:

> Organisations that have fewer accidents than expected balance the tension between rewarding efficiency and rewarding reliability. Firms that have reduced numbers of accidents are fully aware of the simple truth that what gets measured gets managed. They seek to establish reward and incentive systems that balance the costs of potentially unsafe but short-run profitable strategies with the benefits of safe and long-run profitable strategies. They make it politically and economically possible for people to make decisions that are both short-run safe and long-run profitable. This is important to ensure that the focus of the organisation is fixed on accident avoidance. When organisations focus on today's profits without consideration of tomorrow's problems, the likelihood of accidents increases.
>
> (Roberts and Bea, 2001, p. 74)

39

The toolbox

Stakeholder mapping. Stakeholder mapping is a visual process of laying out all stakeholders, their expectations, and their relationships or influences on each other. As a first step, we may brainstorm their power or influence within the organisation, their capacity to take action, their organisational and personal goals, and their opponents or supporters. We need to know where we want them to fit into the organisation.

This brainstorming session may follow the process of visualising. Over the years, a plethora of visualisations of stakeholders have emerged. Per Eden and Ackermann (e.g. 2014), stakeholders can be distinguished by influence/power and interest (see Figure 2.6). Such an analysis may highlight which stakeholders to focus upon, whose buy-in needs to be sought, or whose opinion or view changed.

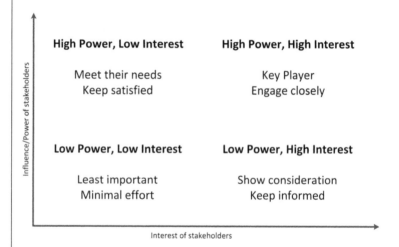

Figure 2.6 Influence/power, interest stakeholder matrix.

Gardner, Rachlin, and Sweeny (1986) produced a power/dynamism matrix. It shows how power/influence may shift over time or the extent to which power can be influenced; thus revealing aspects of predictability (see Figure 2.7).

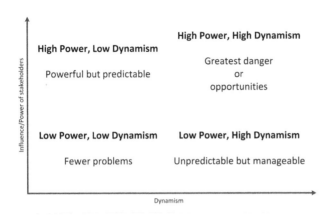

Figure 2.7 Power/dynamism stakeholder matrix (Gardner, Rachlin and Sweeny, 1986).

Benefits mapping. Benefits planning and realisation proclaims to provide a more holistic approach to conventional views that focuses predominantly on the efficient delivery of outputs (e.g. Breese *et al.*, 2015).

Benefits management centres around four principal activities: identification of benefits, analysis of benefits, evaluating their realisation, and assessing their impact in line with the organisation's strategic objectives. The benefits management of an organisation tends to be supported by the process of benefits mapping (see Figure 2.8).

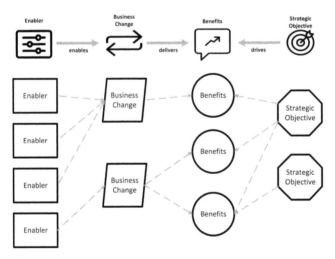

Figure 2.8 Benefits mapping.

There is no single standard for mapping benefits. Primarily, though, the following elements apply in principle to all benefits maps:

- Enabler: physical, tangible entities supporting the business change

- Business change: changes that need to occur in the business/operational environment in order to successfully realise benefits

- Benefits: expected benefits and how these benefits contribute to achieving (weighted) strategic objectives

- Strategic objectives: expression of the organisation's direction (goal, vision, or objective).

Additional aspects may be added to the benefits plan. For example, dis-benefits signify the negative consequences resulting from enablers and business changes.

Clarifying and engaging – Revisiting the development of the Bell-Boeing V-22 Osprey

On 8 April 2000, a V-22 Osprey, an American tilt-rotor aircraft in development, attempted to land at Marana Northwest Regional Airport as part of a training exercise. Upon approach, it suddenly stalled and crashed, killing 19 marines. The Osprey had earned a terrible reputation during development, costing the lives of 32 marines in three crashes.

The idea of an aeroplane that could take off vertically like a helicopter and fly horizontally at high speeds and over long distances was realised by the US Military with the programme to design the Joint Advanced Vertical Lift Aircraft (JVX), led by Bell-Boeing, in 1981.

The programme was plagued with problems from the beginning. The US Army withdrew its commitment in 1987 due to budget constraints, leaving the US Special Ops Command (US SOCOM) as the sole buyer.

The first of six prototypes made its maiden flight in March 1989. Unfortunately, in April 1989, the V-22 programme was cancelled in the 1990 fiscal year's amended budget. Nevertheless, funding and design studies continued, while increasing interest in the Osprey was shown by the US Congress.

The fifth prototype lifted off on 11 June 1991. For observers and the press, this test flight turned out to be a 'rodeo ride'. The Osprey rose into the air, hovered in mid-air, and while trying to land, it violently shrugged to the left and right until its blades hit the ground and disintegrated. House Representative Dave Weldon commented to the Delaware County Daily Times: *"I'd rather it happens now than with Marines on board"* (Whittle, 2010, p. 199).

From July 1992, a string of accidents led to the loss of more marines. In July 1992, nine marines died on board a pre-production V-22; April 2000 saw the biggest loss of life with 19 marines killed during a simulation of a rescue exercise; in December 2000, a V-22 went out of control, killing all four on board.

Despite these tragic setbacks, the developmental testing period showed that the V-22 met or exceeded all performance and handling quality requirements. The combination of speed, range, and vertical take-off capability made it unrivalled as a tilt-rotor concept.

Just-this-way and just-for-now

We may be tempted to seek clarity in direction by banking on what we have been doing well; maintaining the status quo rules out the necessary engagement with stakeholder ambiguity, enabling us to clarify our course of action on the basis of our known success factors. The pursuit of just-this-way provides us with the directness and accuracy to anticipate and respond to incidents early.

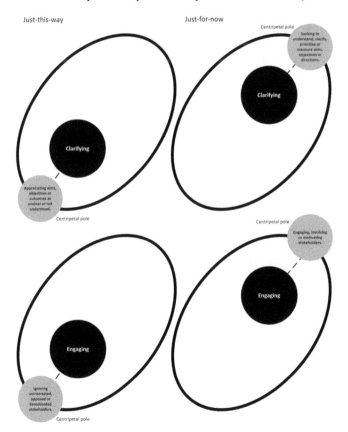

Figure 2.9 Just-this-way and just-for-now polarities (clarifying and engaging).

To explain the lack of reliable performance in the development of the V-22 Osprey (see Figure 2.9), Bell-Boeing stressed their ability to innovate, as they had shown with the predecessor of the V-22, the Boeing Vertol CH-46 Sea Knight. The technological leap to combine a conventional helicopter design with the features of a fixed-wing transport aircraft resulted in a single proposal in February 1983. Just the Bell-Boeing way, this proposal boasted of an engineering marvel. In spite of that, it turned out to be unsafe.

Nevertheless, let's assume, just-for-now, that Bell-Boeing had taken all the US Marines' and US Army's needs into account. The outcome would have exceeded Bell-Boeing's capability to develop a reliable, safe, and functional tilt-rotor aircraft. Ultimately, an even more complex tilt-rotor aircraft, meeting the requirements of all stakeholders, might have meant that the reliability of the V-22 was further jeopardised, with an even greater risk of loss of life than during the development phase.

Just-in-case and just-in-time

To advance our paradoxical thinking (see Figure 2.10), let's reflect upon the benefits and disbenefits that would emerge from the overuse of either pole. On one hand, in light of ambiguous stakeholder expectations, we might look inward and define a course of action based on what we are capable of. Such a view provides stability and anchors the management of the unexpected within the boundaries of what we are good at. Fundamentally, we may ignore some stakeholders who oppose the expectations we are capable of meeting. However, such isolation from stakeholder expectations constrains us to push the boundaries of what is possible. Remaining within the 'safe' boundaries of our expertise, knowledge, and capabilities, we replicate, improve, and perform in a reliable manner but ultimately do not innovate.

On the other hand, we might engage and involve stakeholders to meet as many of their expectations as possible. We reduce ambiguity by clarifying, prioritising, and measuring their expectations and seeking to understand the benefits and dis-benefits. Consequently, we push the envelope beyond what we think we are capable of. This, though, would prompt greater uncertainty and complexity; fewer warning signals would be heeded (see Chapter 3).

As it appears that both poles of the construct of clarifying and engaging yield benefits in anticipating and containing adversity, the following principles may be defined:

JUST-IN-CASE, we are inclined to ignore stakeholders WHILE embracing stakeholder ambiguity. The management of adversity, marked by near-misses and accidents, needs to be treated like a living organism that changes in shape. Although we may draw on our past successes, we need to adapt to stakeholder

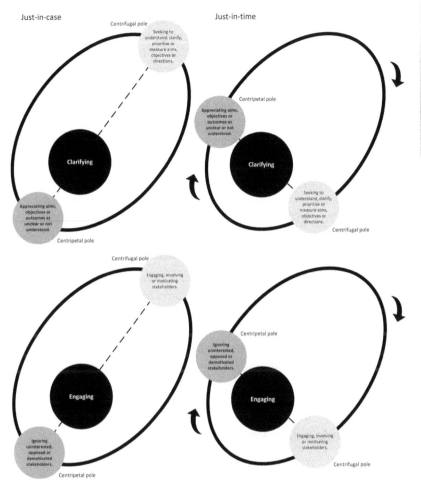

Figure 2.10 Just-in-case way and just-in-time polarities (clarifying and engaging).

ambiguity. Hence, a change in direction should not be seen as a nuisance but as an opportunity to be embraced. It is a constant trade-off, though, between what we think we are good at and what we need to aim for.

JUST-IN-CASE, we want to adapt WHILE maintaining the quality of being reliable. By embracing stakeholder ambiguity, we need to create foresight about how future reliability can be established, maintained, and, most importantly, constantly adapted to the benefits and values that stakeholders deem important. Correspondingly, we need to consider capabilities that enable us to adapt dynamically to the direction we might take while maintaining stability around our organisational critical success factors.

JUST-IN-CASE, we are inclined to appreciate stakeholder ambiguity collectively WHILE owning a temporary resolution of tensions. The management of stakeholder ambiguity should not be reserved solely for those in senior positions. Collectively, all stakeholders should be given some decision-making latitude to address benefits realisation and overcome barriers to our capability to dynamically adapt to the very ambiguity that stakeholders create. This view of collective ownership may well lead to tensions, but they can be addressed through processes of prioritisation, negotiation, and compromise.

From a just-in-case, both/and perspective, we may weigh up the advantages and disadvantages of either pole and determine a novel, well-balanced core definition of the constructs of clarifying and engaging. We may also integrate the construct of clarifying and engaging with another construct, such as controlling (see Chapter 6). The combination and integration of another construct pole would shift the balance around the centripetal and centrifugal poles, just-in-time:

We are inclined to ignore stakeholders WHILE embracing stakeholder ambiguity, AS LONG AS we remain within the boundaries of our ability to influence and control adversity. For all the effort to appreciate and reduce stakeholder ambiguity, if we have little influence or control (see Chapter 6) over activating a response or action or solution, our ability to meet all stakeholders' expectations is in jeopardy. Consequently, just-in-time, our current limitations in controlling adversity demand a balance between reducing and embracing stakeholder ambiguity.

Towards a paradox mindset

By going through the first two steps of paradoxical thinking around the constructs of clarifying and engaging, we may have defined powerful principles that challenge our monolithic, dogmatic thinking about clarifying, prioritising, or measuring aims, objectives, or the direction we want to take in our work unit while we engage with stakeholders. Let's practice those principles; ultimately, we may end up with a principal truth that in itself may not be better or worse than the conventional, centripetal wisdom of ignoring stakeholders altogether and opting to push forwards in a direction that is past-informed and inward-looking.

References

Boynton, A. C. and Zmud, R. W. (1984) 'An assessment of critical success factors', *MIT Sloan Management Review*, 25(4), pp. 17–27.

Breese, R. *et al.* (2015) 'Benefits management: Lost or found in translation', *International Journal of Project Management*, 33(7), pp. 1438–1451.

Bundy, J., Vogel, R. M. and Zachary, M. A. (2018) 'Organization–stakeholder fit: A dynamic theory of cooperation, compromise, and conflict between an organization and its stakeholders', *Strategic Management Journal*, 39(2), pp. 476–501.

Crilly, D. and Sloan, P. (2012) 'Enterprise logic: Explaining corporate attention to stakeholders from the "inside-out"', *Strategic Management Journal*, 33(10), pp. 1174–1193.

Das, T. K. (1991) 'Time: The hidden dimension in strategic planning', *Long Range Planning*, 24(3), pp. 49–57.

Eden, C. and Ackermann, F. (2014) *Making strategy*. London: SAGE Publications.

Eisenhardt, K. M. and Martin, J. A. (2000) 'Dynamic capabilities: What are they?', *Strategic Management Journal*, 21(10–11), pp. 1105–1121.

Flyvbjerg, B. (2008) 'Curbing optimism bias and strategic misrepresentation in planning: Reference class forecasting in practice', *European Planning Studies*, 16(1), pp. 4–21.

Frisch, D. and Baron, J. (1988) 'Ambiguity and rationality', *Journal of Behavioral Decision Making*, 1(3), pp. 149–157.

Gardner, J. R., Rachlin, R. and Sweeny, A. (1986) *Handbook of strategic planning*. New York: John Wiley & Sons, Inc.

Hall, J. and Vredenburg, H. (2005) 'Managing stakeholder ambiguity', *MIT Sloan Management Review*, 47(1), pp. 11–13.

Hart, S. L. and Sharma, S. (2004) 'Engaging fringe stakeholders for competitive imagination', *Academy of Management Executive*, 18(1), pp. 7–18.

Kahneman, D. and Lovallo, D. (2003) 'Delusions of success: How optimism undermines executives' decisions', *Harvard Business Review*, 81(7), pp. 56–63.

Madsen, P. M. (2018) 'Organizing for reliability: a guide for research and practice', in R. Ramanujam & K. H. Roberts (eds.), *Organizing for reliability*. Stanford, CA: Stanford University Press, pp. 143–168.

Roberts, K. H. (1990) 'Managing high reliability organizations', *California Management Review*, 32(4), pp. 101–113.

Roberts, K. H. and Bea, R. (2001) 'Must accidents happen? Lessons from high reliability organizations', *The Academy of Management Executive*, 15(3), pp. 70–79.

Rockart, J. F. (1979) 'Chief executives define their own data needs', *Harvard Business Review*, 57(2), pp. 81–93.

Samuelson, W. and Zeckhauser, R. (1988) 'Status quo bias in decision making', *Journal of Risk and Uncertainty*, 1(1), pp. 7–59.

Waddock, S. A., Bodwell, C. and Graves, S. B. (2002) 'Responsibility: The new business imperative', *Academy of Management Executive*, 16(2), pp. 132–148.

Weick, K. E. (1979) 'Cognitive processes in organizations', in Staw, B. and Cummings, L. (eds.) *Research in organizational behavior*. Greenwich: JAI Press, pp. 41–74.

Weick, K. E. (1995) *Sensemaking in organizations*. Thousand Oaks, CA: Sage Publications.

Weick, K. E. (2015) 'Ambiguity as grasp: The reworking of sense', *Journal of Contingencies and Crisis Management*, 23(2), pp. 117–123.

Whittle, R. (2010) *The dream machine – The untold history of the notorious V-22 Osprey*. New York: Simon & Schuster.

Chapter 3

Heeding warnings or risks

As there is no way of fully predicting and forecasting accidents, let alone near-miss incidents, our futures that we ready and prepare ourselves for remain past-informed (Figure 3.1). In short, we tend to rely on hindsight as a predictor of the future:

> Although the past never repeats itself in detail, it is often viewed as having repetitive elements. People make the same kinds of decisions, face the same kinds of challenges, and suffer the same kinds of misfortune often enough for behavioural scientists to believe that they can detect recurrent patterns.
>
> (Fischhoff, 2002, p. 621)

By surveying the past, we build a foundation to anticipate future adversity by processing the patterns of our behaviours and actions. These recurrent patterns allow us to fill the void of what we believe we do not know about or of what we should or should not do. In principle, our decision-making in the 'here and the now' is retrospective (see Figure 3.1) and we look at current problems from the position of what we have experienced. Past experiences will have led to new skill sets, practices, habits, and routines that we rely upon daily to engage with future warning signals of looming failure. And there lies the problem: our overdependence on hindsight.

Figure 3.1 Foresight through retrospection.

DOI: 10.4324/9781003083115-3

To make matters worse, our capability to heed signals warning of impending adversity is further constrained as there are so many:

> *"Signals are simply viewed as background noise until their meaning is disclosed by an accident"*

> (Perrow, 1984, p. 175)

It is therefore not surprising that the centripetal force of the construct of heeding makes us gravitate towards ignoring and overlooking warning signs demonstrating that we lack the quality of confidently predicting, knowing, or foreseeing (see Figure 3.2).

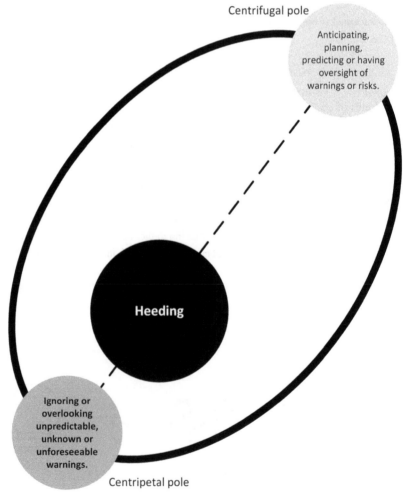

Figure 3.2 Centripetal and centrifugal forces (heeding).

Centripetal wisdom

Hindsight is a double-edged sword. On one hand, it locks our thinking in and, over time, our recollection and retrospective sensemaking of the past are increasingly distorted. On the other hand, it offers useful knowledge if appropriately directed at heeding warning signals of looming incidents.

Our leaning towards ignoring or overlooking warnings of impending adversity is boosted by biases such as normalcy, hindsight, and confirmation bias:

Normalcy. The normalcy bias, or normality bias, makes us underestimate the possibility of an incident or disbelieve warning signals associated with an impending incident (Drabek, 2012). Going hand in hand with the ambiguity effect (see Chapter 2), normalcy bias means that we tend to seize on any ambiguities to justify a more normal and less calamitous assessment of adversity.

Hindsight. Hindsight bias has been one of the most researched decision traps; it encapsulates the tendency to overestimate our ability to foresee and predict the future. It results in overconfidence in our predictions and forecasts and an exaggeration of our ability to analyse warning signals of adversity (Roese and Vohs, 2012).

Confirmation. Confirmation bias makes us lean towards favouring information that confirms opinions and beliefs (Nickerson, 1998). This bias becomes evident when information is recalled selectively to confirm deeply embedded opinions and beliefs, whilst disconfirming and disproving information is downplayed or ignored.

Both confirmation and hindsight bias tend to limit our ability to detect warning signs of impending incidents; in principle hindsight keeps us shackled to thinking and acting in old categories (Langer, 1997). First, any anticipation is directed to the past. Second, the resulting overconfidence in the past as a predictor for the future manifests itself through the dismissal of contrary views.

The toolbox

Risk management. Probabilistic risk assessment methodologies applied in industries such as construction, aerospace, and project planning are advocated as self-evidently correct: as long as one mechanically adheres to probabilistic risk management principles, these methodologies provide confidence in knowing how to mitigate deviations from a planned state. Which of us has not populated a conventional risk register and then participated in, often lengthy, risk review boards?

In principle, a risk management methodology is characterised by activities to identify, assess, and control risks (see Figure 3.3):

Identify exposures to risk	Assess the frequency and severity of these exposures	Implement and adjust control measures

Figure 3.3 Principle steps in risk management.

Identifying legal, regulatory, or commercial risks forms the first step in many traditional risk management methodologies. Their goal is to make visible as many risks as possible. Those risks are then ranked and prioritised, and finally, control measures are implemented to reduce the likelihood and severity of those risks (see Chapter 4).

In recent years, risk management as a standalone process has been embedded in organisational business management frameworks. Most often referred to as Enterprise Risk Management, standards such as ISO 31000 (International Organization for Standardization, 2018) drive organisation-wide implementation of governance principles of continuous improvement.

The benefit of Enterprise Risk Management lies in creating an organisational risk-focused culture grounded in standardised risk reporting and analysis. The extent of risk management standardisation and harmonisation drives transparency, visibility, and consistency in action (see Chapter 5) and thus results in efficiency gains. Beyond efficiency gains, risk management activities can be aligned (see Chapter 7) with the demands of regulatory auditors and examiners.

Heeding the past

Risk management, at its core, draws our attention to the past. It asks us to reassess those repeat experiences as a basis for assessing the likelihood of risk reoccurrence with confidence. It, therefore, reinforces our bias towards relying on the past as a predictor for the future. Yet, while probabilistic risk management comes across as self-evidently correct, its limitations are similarly obvious. The future is anything but certain or straightforward; the lack of historical information undermines any probabilistic risk management tool or technique. In an environment that is characterised by considerable uncertainty (e.g. in innovations), it would be foolish to allow a best-educated guess into a situation where it would mainly reinforce a post-incident judgement of 'I knew it would happen', 'It had to happen', and 'I said it would happen'.

Assumption of normality

"People live as if their expectations are basically correct and as if little can surprise them. To do otherwise would be to forgo any feeling of control or predictability" (Weick and Sutcliffe, 2015, p. 48). Probabilistic risk management boosts our desire to expect the very same we have experienced in the past, as it focuses our minds on those events that we have already experienced and attempted to control. Thus, it confirms and ratifies the past-informed expectations we have about future incidents but fails to challenge our desire for control and predictability or raises doubts about a future we have not yet experienced.

Heeding the process

Much as we tend to recycle our past experiences as a means to predict the future, we may focus our attention more on a process, such as risk management, than on the outputs of such processes. The 'box ticking' mentality (see Chapter 5) confirms an assumption of normality, although the process in itself should tell us that it is anything but normal.

Centrifugal wisdom

The principle concern in probabilistic risk management is the repeatability of incidents in line with their rate of past occurrence. In many cases, probabilities are more guesswork than they are grounded through statistical analysis. Nevertheless, once a probability has been communicated and documented, an estimate may quickly turn into a firm commitment (of normality).

The conventional form of probabilistic risk management, despite its limitations, is one that will stay. Nonetheless, if we want to free ourselves from the shackles of hindsight, we need to start thinking in the 'here and now' as a platform to create foresight. A high-reliability organisation (HRO), as introduced in Chapter 1, tasks every employee, regardless of rank and status, to be vigilant about what *is, may,* or *might* be going wrong. In this respect, it may be noticeable that thinking in the past (e.g. in the shape of lessons learned) is discouraged as we want people to see deviations from a planned state with fresh eyes, in the 'here and now', and not through the lens of hindsight:

> High-reliability managers are always "running scared" with respect of to the problems they are likely to encounter and the ones they have yet to foresee. But they do not rush to conclusions. Their aim is to avoid letting mistakes happen or to work around the ones that have actually occurred in order to

ensure reliability. To do what they need to do, managers have to combine analysis and judgement, a practical draft that resists retrospective validation, let alone prospective formalisation.

(Roe and Schulman, 2008, p. 152)

Vigilance

Being on the lookout for anything that may seem odd, out of the ordinary, different, or fluky requires effort and time. Why maintaining a watchful eye on our activities or other people, if it distracts us from being productive? In practice, we need to be incentivised to maintain a vigilant state of mind and seek out signals of ongoing failure that may translate into a future crisis if left untreated. This requires first that we are given space to zoom out from being task-oriented and use all our senses to make us aware of our surroundings, beyond what our job role tells us to look out for. Second, we need to be stimulated to be uneasy (Reason, 2008) with the ongoing functioning of operations; we need to worry and care about what is at stake:

> If eternal vigilance is the price of liberty, then chronic unease is the price of safety. Studies of [HROs] … indicate that people who operate and manage them tend to assume that each day will be a bad day and act accordingly. But this is not an easy state to sustain, particularly when the thing about which one is uneasy has either not happened, or happened a long time ago, and perhaps to another organisation (Reason, 1997, p. 37).

(in Hopkins, 2009, p. 57)

Vulnerabilities and doubt

We may fail to look out for warning signs if we are not knowledgeable about the environment we are operating in. To 'see' something does not imply that we can attach meaning to it. We need to understand our working environment, processes, and practices to meaningfully connect warning signs with those critical organisational entities threatened by adversity. Vulnerable, critical functions may relate to activities, tasks, processes, or practices for which discontinuance in a reliable manner due to an incident could escalate into a crisis. And it is that vulnerability we need to be aware of and made accountable to (Weick and Sutcliffe, 2015).

The acknowledgement of vulnerabilities in the system goes hand in hand with doubt (Weick and Sutcliffe, 2015) in our capabilities to speedily and effectively anticipate and respond to incidents. Doubt as an unsettled belief drives the apprehension to look constantly for warning signals of impending disaster.

Speaking up

By default, we do not tend to speak about an inconvenient truth or share our concerns about vulnerabilities, inefficiencies, or deviations from what we planned or expected to happen. Hence the following practices are suggested (Detert and Burris, 2016) to encourage speaking up and reporting what could be taken as 'bad news':

Reach out. Instead of waiting until somebody is brave enough to share feedback with us, let us reach out and raise questions that otherwise would not be raised. Employees will appreciate being asked because asking many questions improves interpersonal bonding (Brooks and John, 2018).

Soften the power cues. Critical conversations tend not to cross hierarchical barriers, and thus we may not reach out beyond our role, rank, or status. We need to create an environment that is characterised more by mutual respect and less by authority. Let us address each other by our first names, let others speak first, and do not personalise a concern. Appreciate the message as well as the messenger.

Make feedback a regular, casual exchange. Frequent, informal, face-to-face conversations feel more natural, and barriers towards sharing something perceived as inconvenient and uncomfortable can be broken down. Regardless of the value or validity of somebody's concern, appreciate the person speaking up.

Be transparent. Let us be clear and transparent about the processing of information gathered from these informal conversations. Show what happens with those collected concerns; provide feedback on which ideas are prioritised and, most importantly, what mitigating actions were trigged on the back of the valued employee's feedback.

Such practices will drive encouragement to create a shared sense of alertness about warning signs that may indicate impending adversity. These practices may well be embedded in more formal designated incentives, rewards, and recognition programmes.

Possibilistic thinking

The wealth of information about near-miss incidents and accidents, extracted from every employee in real-time, needs to be analysed, fed back and disseminated to the very same people from whom they were collected. Many foresight methods provide *"alternative scenarios of anticipated futures"* (Weick and Sutcliffe, 2015, p. 126) that take us beyond the realm and law of probabilities, beyond the risk horizon (see Figure 3.4). They make us imagine the possible (Kaplan and Waller, 2018) instead of the probable – outcomes that we have yet to experience – but also allow us to heed warning signals we would not otherwise normally pay attention to.

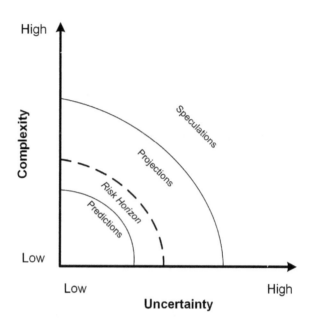

High

Complexity

Low

Low   High
Uncertainty

Speculations

Projections

Risk Horizon

Predictions

Figure 3.4 Heeding beyond the risk horizon.

Background noise

The heeding of context-based information will result in a sea of signals that we may drown in. The first challenge is to pick out those warnings of impending adversity and the second is not to oversimplify them and treat them in isolation. Instead, interpretive vigilance (Macrae, 2009) requires scrutinising patterns, drawing connections, the recognition of novelty, and sensing discrepancies, for example, between the emergence of warning signals in the past and the current context (see the next toolbox).

The toolbox

Scenario planning. While scenario planning has its origins in military strategy studies, it was transformed into a business tool by, among others, Wack (e.g. 1985) and Schoemaker (e.g. 1995). In contrast to risk management, which drives the anticipation of individual risks, scenario planning caters for multiple future realities and encourages thinking to the extremes of both the possible and the plausible.

Scenario planning aims to define a group of possible and plausible (not necessarily probable) futures that should constructively challenge each other. Compared with traditional risk management, this approach does not aim to focus attention on quantifying a single future; instead, it provides multiple, more abstract projections of alternative futures:

> Firms develop a combination of scenarios that create a hypotheti-cal exogenous shock. The scenario planning team then formulates contingencies for handling the shock, employing a "learning before doing" simulation (Pisano, 1994). Table top exercises are a common method used by leading managers to walk-through the hypothetical scenarios, listing actions needed at each step of the incident response (Cavanagh, 2008). Eventually, the firm compares current organisa-tional routines with the proposed emergency responses. Ideally, core routines within the firm are modified in anticipation of possible shock scenarios to establish resilience within the normal workflow of the firm (Gersick, 1991).

> (Worthington, Collins, and Hitt, 2009, p. 444)

Scenario planning is a powerful tool if applied in a non-threatening environ-ment. For scenario planning to take effect, the culture of a project needs to be 'open-minded' with:

1. Receptiveness to multiple, sometimes divergent, perspectives.
2. Openness to having one's views questioned and challenged.
3. The use of a leader or facilitator who can manage the process of sce-nario planning in a controlled but non-threatening manner.
4. Willingness to provide resources to deal with essential issues that may occur.
5. Acknowledgement that scenarios are uncertain in their predic-tive power and that the 'truth' will not be forthcoming through this technique.

The starting point (see Figure 3.5) of scenario planning involves devising a problem statement – a concise description of the problem. This is fol-lowed by the mapping of critical drivers that influence the problem state-ment. The drivers may be mapped in line with variables such as uncertainty and uncontrollability. Choosing the most uncontrollable and most uncertain drivers informs a polarity map that includes extreme positive and extreme negative forms of these two most critical drivers. For each of the four sce-narios, a short story is written, as it has been found that organisational stories effectively capture the imagination and give issues far more imme-diacy (Denning, 2004). Finally, developing a catchy name for each scenario sticks in the mind and captures the essence of each one.

Define Problem Statement	Identify Critical Uncertainties
Develop Plausible Scenarios Polarity Mapping	Discuss Implications Story telling

X
Y
Z

1 2
3 4

Figure 3.5 Principal process of scenario planning.

Delphi method. The Delphi technique constitutes a systematic, interactive action-oriented method that relies on a panel of experts. Its origin lies in the defence; "Project Delphi" was a US Air Force-sponsored RAND (standing for research and development) corporation study. Its principal aim was to obtain a consensus among a group of experts (Ogbeifun, Mbohwa, and Pretorius, 2017).

In principle, a Delphi undergoes distinct phases (see Figure 3.6). As with scenario planning, the first phase revolves around defining a problem statement; each expert contributes to the problem statement's formulation and diagnosis. Rounds of questions then follow the definition of a problem statement. In the first round, we need to pose general questions to comprehend the specialists and their perspectives about future events. Following rounds may reveal significant disagreement; then that disagreement is explored to bring out the underlying rationales for these differences to be analysed. In the last round, a final evaluation takes place when all evaluations have been fed back for consideration and an agreement has been arrived at.

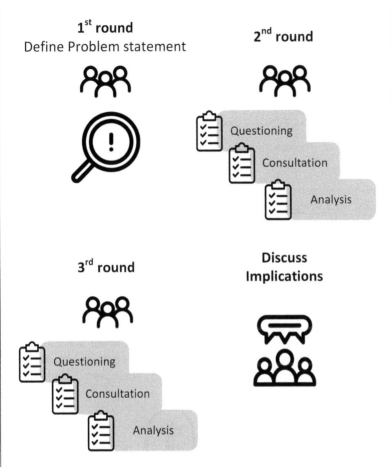

1st round
Define Problem statement

2nd round

Questioning

Consultation

Analysis

3rd round

Questioning

Consultation

Analysis

**Discuss
Implications**

Figure 3.6 Principal process of the Delphi technique.

Horizon scanning. Another foresight technique (see Figure 3.7), a horizon scan, draws on detecting early signals that influence and impact the current environment. The principle premise of horizon scanning is to identify causal links and loops that demonstrate persistent problems and trends. It challenges assumptions about constancy and dynamism in the environment.

Horizon scanning tends to be based on desk research, loosely defined as the collection of secondary data. Sources range from the internet and online databases to data from government and non-governmental organisations. Another means of locating sources for horizon scanning is direct contact with experts at the forefront in the area of concern.

Exploration
Define Problem Statement

Scanning

Discuss
Implications

Figure 3.7 Principal process of horizon scanning.

Horizon scanning incorporates aspects of both Delphi and scenario plan-ning. As outlined by the Delphi method, expert panels may contribute to a reliable horizon scan. The definition of trends that enhances the scenario planning process may provide an early indicator of which scenario is mate-rialising (Rowe, Wright, and Derbyshire, 2017).

Pre-mortem. A pre-mortem (see Figure 3.8) is a tool to make us imagine, for example, how a project that we have not yet engaged with will fail. In a backward-oriented process, we then determine what potentially leads to a worst-case scenario. Similar to scenario planning, introduced in Chapter 2, a pre-mortem enables us to uncover blind spots in our anticipation of impending incidents. Besides, a pre-mortem fosters open communication, addresses a fear of failure, and drives a healthy scepticism:

Figure 3.8 A pre-mortem.

It also reduces the kind of damn-the-torpedoes attitude often assumed by people who are overinvested in a project. Moreover, in describing weaknesses that no one else has mentioned, team members feel valued for their intelligence and experience, and others learn from them. The exercise also sensitises the team to pick up early signs of trouble once the project gets underway. In the end, a premortem may be the best way to circumvent any need for a painful postmortem.

(Klein, 2007, p. 1)

Commencing a pre-mortem assumes that a worst-case scenario has hypothetically already materialised. Participants are allowed to express their perspective of extreme failure, the assumed inability to prevent or contain incidents in the first place.

The next step is to explore why this imaginary worst-case might have materialised. In line with some aspects of scenario planning, contributing factors to failure may be categorised in terms of the extent of their certainty and controllability; the reasoning behind each factor should be captured.

Once the biggest 'show-stoppers' are in the open, some time can be spent reviewing all worst-case perspectives and trajectories; multiple pre-mortem stories may emerge that require different preventative and containing approaches.

Heeding – Revisiting the demise of Kodak

In January 2012, Kodak, an American technology company that concentrated on imaging products and had invented the hand-held camera, filed for bankruptcy. What was once considered a hub of technological wizardry suddenly became an institution with little hope of surviving much longer into the future.

The demise of Kodak, like nothing else, highlights the ongoing need for top-level managers to cope with the effects of uncertainty. The use of photographic film was pioneered by George Eastman, who started manufacturing paper film in 1885 before switching to celluloid in 1889. His first camera, which he called the 'Kodak', was first offered for sale in 1888. It was a very simple box camera with a fixed-focus lens and single shutter speed, which, along with its relatively low price, appealed to the average consumer. The first camera using digital electronics to capture and store images was developed by 1975. The adoption of digital cameras was slow. In 1999, with the rise of broadband technology to share digital images, the demand for stand-alone digital cameras exploded, fuelled by the introduction of the iPhone in 2007. The volatility in the environment, amplified by the rise of the smartphone, caught Kodak off guard, partly because of its lack of understanding of market volatility:

Kodak's top management never fully grasped how the world around them was changing. They hung on to now obsolete assumptions about who took pictures, why and when.

(Munir, 2016)

Just-this-way and just-for-now

Recent generations of Kodak managers rested on the laurels of having been the leader in the imaging and photography industry. For years, they downplayed external competition and innovations as non-threatening. Although signals of the emergence of digital photography were abundant, they were not heeded. Why should they be? Instead, a state of normality was assumed until it was too late (see Figure 3.9).

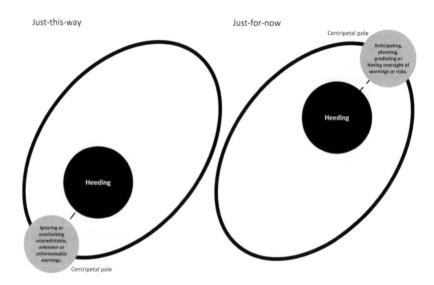

Just-this-way

Just-for-now

Centripetal pole

Anticipating, planning, predicting or having oversight of warnings or risks.

Heeding

Heeding

Ignoring or overlooking unpredictable, unknown or unforeseeable warnings.

Centripetal pole

Figure 3.9 Just-this-way and just-for-now polarity (heeding).

To adopt the opposite pole to ignoring or overlooking warning signals, just-for-now, Kodak would have had to abandon the tried and tested technology that had served them so well over the years. Instead, they would have had to look outwards and listen to and consider an infinite amount of information about new technologies that lacked the confirmatory power to persuade them to abandon an established technology. Why fix a winning formula, if it is not yet broken?

Just-in-case and just-in-time

The heedful anticipation of impending adversity is essentially retrospective (Weick, 1995). We tend to be bound by the past, our view of the future is intrinsically shaped and framed by our past experiences. In this respect, by default, there is a strong leaning towards the use of deterministic, probabilistic routines, and assessments. Our innate propensity towards exploiting the confirmatory power of hindsight as a predictor for the future is reinforced by toolsets (e.g. probabilistic risk management) that are advocated as self-evidently correct. As a consequence, we largely heed those warning signals that we have experienced before, that we are familiar and comfortable with; and thus ignore other information that we are doubtful about or perceive as uncertain or ambiguous (see Chapter 2). Let's challenge such centripetal wisdom and engage with balancing both gravitational poles (see Figure 3.10), by looking at (dis)benefits.

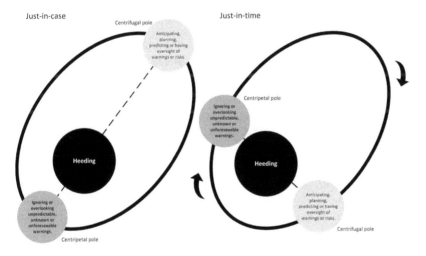

Figure 3.10 Just-in case way and just-in-time polarity (heeding).

On one hand, we tend to rely on the abundance of evidence that the past brings with it, just-in-case the future repeats itself on the back of our past successes and failures. We can heed warning signals that we can measure probabilistically (see Chapter 4). Nevertheless, our breadth and depth of heeding are limited to what has happened repeatedly in the past. Novelty in the environment is not heeded and, consequently, blind spots emerge.

On the other hand, just-for-now, we may detach ourselves from the past and venture beyond the tangible, the measurable, and the familiar. We try to heed any possible threat and pay attention to an infinite number of warning signals in real-time. Instead of relying on the past, we create an organisational awareness of the 'here and now'. Nonetheless, the endless flow of information about impending adversity is challenged by a limited capacity to process such information, to distinguish mere noise from relevant data. We could play catch up, trying to process real-time information while incidents keep derailing our reliable performance.

Again, as in Chapter 2, we are faced with two simultaneous opposites that seem to be equally (un)favourable or (un)satisfactory. Ergo, just-in-case, let's have a bit of both, putting both centripetal and centrifugal wisdom in place:

JUST-IN-CASE, we tend to analyse past experiences WHILE second-guess them. We need to listen to our inner voice, whether we have seen something like this incident in the past, and how we responded to it. We have to educate ourselves and others about the risk of relying on hindsight and create awareness about the risk of hindsight bias and the use of tools and techniques that reinforce the dependence on hindsight. Let's doubt our first inclination to think and act in the past.

JUST-IN-CASE, we are inclined to predict and forecast the future WHILE readying ourselves for deviations in real time. We should not assume that the tools of foresight that have been described are about predicting or forecasting the future. They advocate the challenging of past-informed and shaped mindsets in order to raise questions about what we do not know, rather than about what we expect to know about the future. In this regard, these tools may make people uncomfortable because they reveal that the future is not like the past but multifaceted, complex, and unknown. Scenario planning, a Delphi and horizon scanning are only some of many foresight tools. We should not simply educate others to apply those tools mindlessly. We should have critical conversations about how much these tools rely on hindsight and how much true foresight is created that will enable us to transcend our past experiences.

JUST-IN-CASE, we prefer to plan for a single future WHILE considering multiple perspectives. Regardless of the outcomes of hindsight or foresight-based tools, they will all be framed differently. We should appreciate different and conflicting perspectives, as well as resist the temptation to create an illusion of certainty and control by merely ignoring other views.

JUST-IN-CASE, we are predisposed to pay heed to a best-case scenario WHILE being vigilant about the emergence of a worst-case scenario. It is important that we keep oversight of what we are accomplishing, and which milestones we have met. At the same time, we must be vigilant about what we have not yet accomplished. Even if we feel we are close to realising a best case, we will have to remain on the lookout for cues that indicate a worsening performance.

The process of heeding warning signals may simply be a question of integrating centripetal and centrifugal wisdom into novel principles of anticipating and containing near-miss incidents and accidents. In addition, we may take other construct poles into account that shape the core definition of heeding, by for example, allowing the process of simplifying (see Chapter 4) to tip the balance of heeding, just-in-time, towards the unconventional, less obvious, and less self-evidently correct centrifugal pole:

We tend to analyse past experiences WHILE second-guessing them, AS LONG AS we are not oversimplifying. This principle implies that we constantly update our contextual awareness of the 'here and now', being guided about what we have experienced but unwilling to give in to the temptation to think in old categories (Langer and Beard, 2014) and to jump to conclusions. The condition of oversimplification informs the extent to which we continue to heed warning signals of our own assumptions and apply interpretive scrutiny to these warning signals (see Chapter 4).

Towards a paradox mindset

As a consequence of the above process of heeding, of simultaneous retrospection and anticipation, we may define operating principles that constantly leave us in a healthy limbo about what warning signals to heed and what to ignore. In the end, this may well lead towards cognitive overload, and our process of heeding will become less favourable than our possible starting point, focussing on either a centripetal or a centrifugal pole. Once you have defined your principles, articulate them, turn them into practice, and feel and experience them.

References

Brooks, A. W. and John, L. K. (2018) 'The surprising power of questions', *Harvard Business Review*, 96(3), pp. 60–67.

Cavanagh, T. M. (2008) *Benchmarking business preparedness: Plans, procedures, and implementation of standards*. New York: The Conference Board.

Denning, S. (2004) 'Telling tales', *Harvard Business Review*, 82(5), pp. 122–129.

Detert, J. and Burris, E. (2016) 'Can your employees really speak freely?', *Harvard Business Review*, 41(7), pp. 40–50.

Drabek, T. E. (2012) *Human system responses to disaster: An inventory of sociological findings*. New York: Springer.

Fischhoff, B. (2002) 'For those condemned to study the past: Heuristics and biases in hindsight', in Levitin, D. J. (ed.) *Foundations of cognitive psychology*. Cambridge, MA: MIT Press, pp. 621–636.

Gersick, C. J. G. (1991) 'Revolutionary change theories: A multilevel exploration of the punctuated equilibrium paradigm', *The Academy of Management Review*, 16(1), pp. 10–36.

Hopkins, A. (2009) 'Identifying and responding to warnings', in Hopkins, A. (ed.) *Learning from high reliability organisations*. North Ryde: CCH Australia, pp. 33–58.

International Organization for Standardization (2018) *Risk Management ISO 31000*. Geneva.

Kaplan, S. and Waller, M. J. (2018) 'Reliability through resilience in organizational teams', in Ramanujam, R. and Roberts, K. H. (eds.) *Organizing for reliability: A guide for research and practice*. Stanford, CA: Stanford University Press.

Klein, G. (2007) 'Performing a project premortem', *Harvard Business Review*, 85(9), pp. 18–19.

Langer, E. and Beard, A. (2014) 'Mindfulness in the age of complexity', *Harvard Business Review*, 92(3), pp. 68–73.

Langer, E. J. (1997) *The power of mindful learning*. Reading, MA: Addison-Wesley.

Macrae, C. (2009) 'From risk to resilience: Assessing flight safety incidents in airlines', in Hopkins, A. (ed.) *Learning from high reliability organisations*. North Ryde: CCH Australia, pp. 95–115. https://www.google.de/books/edition/Learning_from_High_Reliability_Organisat/9KfiwAEACAAJ?hl=de

Munir, K. (2016) 'The demise of Kodak: Five reasons', *Wall Street Journal*. http://blogs.wsj.com/source/2012/02/26/the-demise-of-kodak-five-reasons/.

Nickerson, R. (1998) 'Confirmation bias: A ubiquitous phenomenon in many guises', *Review of General Psychology*, 2(2), pp. 175–220.

Ogbeifun, E., Mbohwa, C. and Pretorius, J. H. C. (2017) *Achieving consensus devoid of complicity: Adopting the Delphi Technique*. Bingley: Emerald.

Perrow, C. (1984) *Normal accidents*. New York: Basic Books.

Pisano, G. P. (1994) 'Knowledge, integration, and the locus of learning: An empirical analysis of process development', *Management Journal*, 15(2), pp. 85–100.

Reason, J. (1997) *Managing the risks of organisational accidents*. Aldershot: Ashgate.

Reason, J. (2008) *The human contribution: Unsafe acts, accidents and heroic recoveries*. Boca Raton, FL: Taylor & Francis.

Roe, E. and Schulman, P. R. (2008) *High reliability management: Operating on the edge*. Stanford, CA: Stanford University Press (High reliability and crisis management).

Roese, N. J. and Vohs, K. D. (2012) 'Hindsight bias', *Perspectives on Psychological Science*, 7(5), pp. 411–426.

Rowe, E., Wright, G. and Derbyshire, J. (2017) 'Enhancing horizon scanning by utilizing pre-developed scenarios: Analysis of current practice and specification of a process improvement to aid the identification of important "weak signals"', *Technological Forecasting and Social Change*, 125, pp. 224–235.

Schoemaker, P. (1995) 'Scenario planning: A tool for strategic thinking', *Sloan Management Review*, 36(2), pp. 25–40.

Wack, P. (1985) 'Scenarios: Unchartered waters ahead', *Harvard Business Review*, 63(5), pp. 73–89.

Weick, K. and Sutcliffe, K. (2015) *Managing the unexpected: Sustained performance in a complex world*. 3rd edn. Hoboken, NJ: Wiley.

Weick, K. E. (1995) *Sensemaking in organizations*. Thousand Oaks, CA: Sage Publications.

Worthington, W. J., Collins, J. D. and Hitt, M. A. (2009) 'Beyond risk mitigation: Enhancing corporate innovation with scenario planning', *Business Horizons*, 52(5), pp. 441–450.

Chapter 4

Simplifying problems, solutions, or responses

Chapter 3 focused on our ignorance of the future, the lack of complete certainty that hampers our ability to anticipate the emergence of near-misses and accidents. To make matters more challenging for us, the future is not only uncertain but also complex, resulting in countless interrelated factors that we need to disentangle as a prerequisite for a clear and focused response.

To make decisions and move forward, we must simplify the complex. In short, we simplify data and information about the warning signals (see Figure 4.1) that we have chosen to heed (see Chapter 3):

> All organisations must simplify the data which confront them in order to make decisions and move forward. Simplification means discarding some information as unimportant or irrelevant. But this is inherently dangerous, for the discarded information may be the very information to avert disaster.
>
> (Hopkins, 2009, p. 12)

Figure 4.1 Simplifying.

67

DOI: 10.4324/9781003083115-4

The process of simplification, tempting as it might be in creating clarity for our decision-making (see Chapter 5), can be detrimental to our ability to anticipate adversity, as discarding data and information *"increase[s] the likelihood of eventual surprise"* (Weick and Sutcliffe, 2001, p. 94).

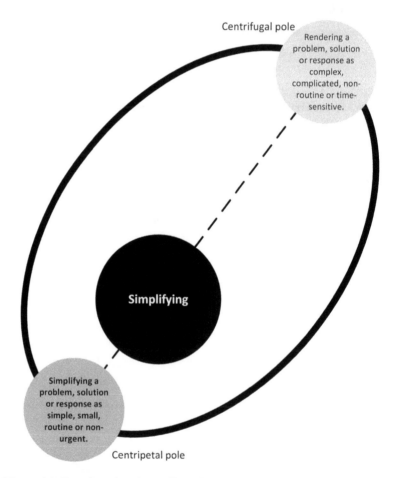

Figure 4.2 Centripetal and centrifugal forces (simplifying).

As shown in Figure 4.2, we tend to render near-miss incidents and accidents as simple, small, routine, or non-urgent so we can move on. Centripetal wisdom indicates a longing for simplicity, which goes together with our tendency to reduce or ignore stakeholder ambiguity (see Chapter 2) and warning signals (see Chapter 3). The process of simplification is amplified over time as we develop an understanding of adversity:

Simplification comes into play when that "stream of cues" changes and the course of action changes. Once you form a hunch of what is happening, you may put less weight on any cue that comes later. When you put less weight on subsequent cues, that lesser weight does not distinguish between cues that suggest the diagnosis is wrong and cues that suggest it's correct.

(Weick and Sutcliffe, 2015, p. 71)

 ## Centripetal wisdom

In conjunction with the need to make sense of a world full of stakeholder ambiguity and an infinite number of warning signals, we may fall prey to the lure of oversimplification. Inherent complexity may be downgraded to being something that is at most simple. Amplified by a focus on hindsight (see Chapter 3), the complexity of near-misses and actual incidents may be reduced to the illusory belief that we have established a clear cause for an agreed symptom and also arrived at a definite solution. As a result, we present it as non-urgent or straightforward enough so that we can move on:

Representativeness heuristic. The representativeness heuristic is a mental shortcut that amplifies our propensity to simplify decisions:

> A person who follows this heuristic evaluates the probability of an uncertain event, or a sample, by the degree to which it is: (i) similar in essential properties to its parent population; and (ii) reflects the salient features of the process by which it is generated. Our thesis is that, in many situations, an event A is judged more probable than an event B whenever A appears more representative than B. In other words, the ordering of events by their subjective probabilities coincides with their ordering by representativeness.

(Kahneman and Tversky, 1972, p. 431)

As a consequence of this heuristic contributing to the manifestations of other biases (e.g. hindsight bias, confirmation bias, etc.), we may overestimate our ability to anticipate near-misses and accidents.

The toolbox

In the previous chapter (see Figure 3.3), the process of probabilistic risk management was introduced and scrutinised in the context of drawing our attention to the past. Probabilistic risk management, representative of many other tools, techniques, and processes to address future adversity, will be in the spotlight again in this chapter. This time, though, the process step of risk assessment is dissected in relation to its disposition of oversimplification (see Figure 4.3).

Identify exposures
to risk

**Assess the
frequency and
severity of these
exposures**

Implement and adjust
control measures

Figure 4.3 Risk assessment.

Risk assessment. The process step of risk assessment (see Figure 4.4) relies on two principle quantities: the likelihood or probability of occurrence and the magnitude or severity; in short: Risk = Likelihood × Impact.

Impact

Likelihood	Negligible	Minor	Moderate	Major	Catastrophic
Almost certain	Moderate	High	Extreme	Extreme	Extreme
Likely	Moderate	High	High	Extreme	Extreme
Possible	Low	Moderate	High	High	Extreme
Unlikely	Low	Moderate	Moderate	High	High
Rare	Low	Low	Low	Moderate	Moderate

Figure 4.4 Risk matrix.

This equation of likelihood multiplied by impact allows us to focus our attention on those risks with a quotient that conveys high certainty of the incident occurring and a significant potential impact.

The analysis of risks often takes place in an organisation during the planning stage. Lengthy risk registers that are evaluated and approved by risk review boards are not uncommon. Such planning also includes answers about how to respond to those risks. In principle, risks can be transferred, avoided, retained, or controlled. A risk transfer response implies that the risk exposure is transferred to another party. Avoiding risk may involve not performing the task with which the risk is associated. Retaining a risk is usually an option where the costs of mitigating the risk outweigh the benefits or rewards of engaging with the risky undertaking. Finally, risk control refers to a targeted response to reduce the likelihood of a risk occurring and reduce its severity.

Root cause assessment. Whereas a risk assessment is carried out ahead of any materialisation of adversity, a root cause identification and assessment is usually done afterwards, as an integral part of an investigation or lessons learned workshop.

A root cause analysis assists in identifying how and why an adverse incident occurred. Derived from quality control, a tool commonly used for determining the root causes of quality problems is a Fishbone Diagram (Juran and De Feo, 2010), as displayed in Figure 4.5.

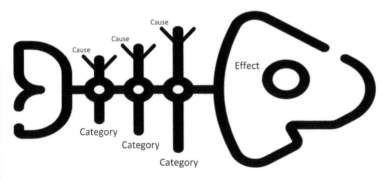

Figure 4.5 Fishbone diagram.

In an iterative process, major categories of causes for a problem are determined. These categories are then, in turn, broken down into possible individual causes. Once all causes are identified and all cause-effect relationships exhausted, then corrective measures can be identified.

Oversimplification

Our minds are constantly bombarded with a tremendous amount of information. As a result, we turn to the age-old coping mechanism of simplifying the world around us. In just this spirit, conventional risk assessment draws on simplified hindsight as a predictor for the future (see Chapter 3). As described before, probabilistic risk management asks us to identify risks associated with a plan; it asks us to evaluate risks in isolation. As a result, relying on a simple risk register/matrix has its limitations, as it

- does not easily allow causes to be linked with specific risk controls;

- does not easily show which risk controls apply to more than one cause;

- does not usually allow for more than one outcome;

- does not show which causes are the biggest contributors to risk;

- encourages risk reduction by adding extra controls, rather than improving existing risk controls; and

- draws the focus to assessing the level of risk for each perceived [risk], often at the expense of properly assessing the effectiveness of controls in managing the risk (Bice and Hayes, 2009, p. 63).

Consequently, we may believe that we are in control of a risk just because we have been able to identify and articulate it, associate a probability and impact with confidence, and allocate a response to this single risk. But essentially, the process of risk management may merely provide us with an oversimplified illusion of present and future adversity.

Lack of focus

"Risk matrices work only if the consequence and frequency assessments are referring to the same scenario" (Hayes, 2009, p. 129); and such scenarios might be mundane, not affecting critical functions or safety-sensitive issues. Hence, based on a mere probability/impact analysis, we may focus our attention on risks regardless of the outcome that the scenario relates, heedless (see Chapter 3) of the significance of the context to which the risk is associated.

Testing the past

Due to the emphasis on probabilities, we form tentative explanations of past events to be tested by further investigation in the form of risk management controls. But while we are focusing our attention on reanalysing the past, near-miss incidents and accidents might already be happening in the 'here and now' (see Chapter 3). Therefore, assumptions of emerging adversity that are sometimes aired as doubt or unease would not make it onto a risk register, as we could not associate them with a probability.

Single-point estimates

A risk assessment as described above results in single-point values assigned to individual risks. Although these single-point estimates serve as best guesses, they are all too often framed as single-point commitments. Even when we come up with, for example, multiple probabilities, we are tempted to reduce them to take for granted single-point averages that then become set-in-stone commitments.

Single attribution

Our behaviour in relation to single-point estimates for individual risks resembles what happens with single attribution of responsibilities. Once we have simplified the occurrence and impact of a risk, we add to it the contribution individuals can make to avoid, mitigate, transfer, escalate (see Chapter 6), or accept the risk. As a consequence, not only are risks identified and assessed in isolation of each other but so also is the response to them.

Manageability

The initial risk assessment that we carry out sets the scene for how manageable we frame the future to be. This focal point is rarely adjusted and our decision-making is essentially biased towards the initial simplified estimates. Hence, a constant interplay between simplification and anchoring bias (see Chapter 2) drives a static perception of risk and overoptimistic expectations of the manageability of near-misses and accidents.

Anchoring

Conventional, probabilistic risk management sets the scene for our actions. Just as a risk register makes us simplify an understanding of current and future adversity, it also anchors our expectations for managing adversity by wedding us to the past: *"A self-fulfilling interpretation is created, an interpretation that becomes further and further removed from the data"* (Weick and Sutcliffe, 2015, p. 71).

Centrifugal wisdom

To make sense of a complex world, we need to simplify and create order amid the complexity. We are turning the complex into the simple, something that can be broken down into its parts, which can be addressed in isolation of each other. However, our longing for simplicity leads us away from a nuanced understanding of impending adversity; it limits, if not reduces, our ability to anticipate adversity early. To counter the temptation to oversimplify,

> HROs take deliberate steps to create a more complete and nuanced picture of what they face and who they are as they face it. Knowing that the world they face is complex, unstable unknowable, and unpredictable, HROs position themselves to see as much as possible.

(Weick and Sutcliffe, 2007, p. 10)

To 'see as much as possible', plural viewpoints on events are encouraged and a closer focus on context is sought. In essence, greater scrutiny is exercised in the process of simplifying the threat of a crisis or disaster foreshadowed by near-miss incidents and accidents. It is simply not taken for granted that the past will replicate itself item by item and that we can break down that past into its parts so we can manage them in isolation from each other.

Scepticism

The acknowledgement that something is not going well often goes hand in hand with the definition of surface explanations of why failure persists despite our efforts to prevent it from materialising in the first place. Hence, when we come across signals of simplifications, such as overhearing somebody saying that 'it is not a problem', we are reluctant to accept them but probe their justification; we dig deeper until we can assess whether the isolated problem constitutes a systemic issue that, if left untreated, intensifies (Weick and Sutcliffe, 2006).

Communication

Tools and techniques not only magnify the appeal of simplification but also how we exchange information and rely on symbols, signs, and behaviours. This requires us to pay attention to how we communicate. As outlined in Chapter 8, to confront oversimplifications, we need to rely on open, transparent, and honest sharing of information to turn data into meaningful big pictures (see Chapter 7) that are updated in real-time.

Focus on control mechanisms

From a perspective of probabilistic risk management, we reduce future adversity into individual risks that are assessed and prioritised by the likelihood of occurrence and impact. Therefore, the focus of our attention is on the risk, and less on controlling the risk. Nevertheless, we may oversimplify both the risk and our ability to prevent it from happening or reduce its potential impact. Thus, control and response mechanisms need to be scrutinised as much as the existence of the risk itself.

The here and now

Although our management of adversity is essentially retrospective (see Chapter 3), we still focus our minds on the here and now, updating our interpretation of adversity in real-time:

> With closer attention to context comes more differentiation of worldviews and mindsets. And with more differentiation comes a richer and more varied picture of potential consequences, which in turns suggests a richer and more varied set of precautions and early warning signs.
>
> (Weick and Sutcliffe, 2007, p. 53)

Henceforth, we need to be sceptical about the assumptions we make about the future, about how far our simplified interpretation of the world matches our present context and whether our simplification is just a duplication of our past experiences.

Burden of proof

Relying on hindsight provides us with facts and evidence and, translated by probabilities, helps us to convey confidence in our predictions, however wrong they turn out to be in an environment that is anything but certain. This leaves us with the problem of making a case for challenging and questioning our assumptions in the light of what we do not know about the future. The onus of proof cannot be on the one questioning and challenging. In other words, in challenging somebody else's simplification shaped by past experiences and expectations of normality (see Chapter 3), we have no proof, as the future is always unproven until it materialises. Consequently, to challenge our simplified assumptions and expectations about the future, the burden of proof needs to be reduced, if not eliminated. Instead, increased scrutiny through challenging and questioning by sceptics is a leap of faith.

The toolbox

Bow-ties. Figure 4.6 offers a glimpse of a bow-tie. In highlighting the digressions from conventional risk registers and matrices (see the previous toolbox), the aspect of probabilities in bow-ties is not one of the dominant variables; the dominant variables are causes, controls, and escalation factors (Bice and Hayes, 2009).

As a first step in developing a bow-tie, a top event is identified and analysed in terms of its significance. It is an undesirable event that needs to be prevented in the first place, and if that is unsuccessful, it must be contained. This step is followed by mapping out direct causes:

> The directness is important, as this is a good test to determine whether the threat is truly a threat or perhaps a failed control. For example, will air traffic controller fatigue cause two aircrafts to come into close proximity, or will it defeat air traffic controller skill and cause an error of instruction to the pilot?" Clearly, the latter is true, so air traffic controller error is the threat rather than fatigue.

> (Bice and Hayes, 2009, p. 67)

The third step in the process of a bow-tie assessment is the identification, classification, and evaluation of barriers to prevent near-miss incidents from being ignored, thus leading to a race to the top event. In addition, if the top event materialises due to the failure of preventative barriers to take hold, recovery mechanisms are defined to prevent a cascade into an irrecoverable disaster.

The bow-tie analysis can be further enhanced by focussing on escalation factors. Those may refer to conditions that increase or intensify the speed or extent to which causal factors result in the top event or prevent us from containing the top event.

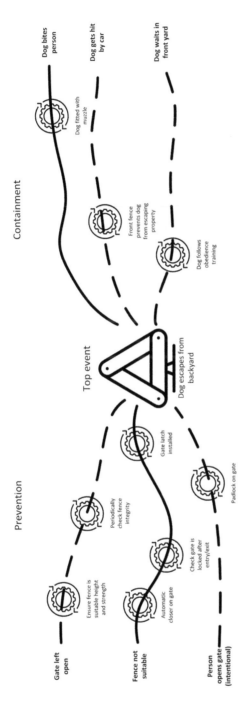

Figure 4.6 An example of a bow-tie (adapted from Bice and Hayes, 2009, p. 73).

Four Ways of Seeing. The Four Ways of Seeing technique (Hoffman, 2017) provides multiple perspectives (see Figure 4.7) on a subject such as impending adversity.

In combination with the identification of different perspectives of stakeholders (see Chapter 2), the process starts with an assessment of how we see ourselves. This may well include the question of how we assess our ability to anticipate and prepare for incidents that may jeopardise the realisation of those benefits we deem most important (see Chapter 2 for Benefits mapping). Then, moving to the lower-left quadrant, we may explore our perception of other stakeholders' readiness and preparedness for adversity. Ending up with the lower-right quadrant, we can identify blind spots and tensions that need addressing.

Figure 4.7 Four ways of seeing (Hoffman, 2017, p. 178).

Storytelling. Going back to our childhood, stories are principal, primal forms of communication. They have grabbed our attention and provided us with meaning at an age when we have little experience to rely on. Our brains are hardwired for stories. They help us make sense of our environment and simplify the complexity that we encounter on a daily basis.

Effective stories (Ready, 2002) are those that are context-specific; they relate directly to the context the listeners find themselves in. Other contexts, for the purpose of comparing and contrasting, may be added, but the essence of a story is contextualised in the reality of the listener. Furthermore, the most powerful stories are those told by role models who have experienced them first-hand. Those in high standing are more likely to be listened to, and hearing it from the 'horse's mouth' adds to the originality and authenticity of the story. Finally, and not least, drama in a story enhances the learning effect and builds empathy towards the storyteller.

Socratic questioning. We may facilitate a meaningful dialogue through Socratic questioning. Socratic questioning is widely used in teaching and counselling. In principle, it helps to expose and challenge deeply held values, beliefs, and assumptions. The following questions (see Figures 4.8 and 4.9) may provide us with a structure that challenges our propensity towards oversimplification:

**Keeping Participants Focused on
The Elements of Thought**

Did the questioner make the goal of the discussion clear? (What is the goal of this discussion? What are we trying to accomplish?)

Did the questioner pursue relevant information? (What information are you basing that comment on? What experience convinced you of this?)

Did the questioner question inferences, interpretations, and conclusions where appropriate or significant? (How did you reach that conclusion? Could you explain your reasoning? Is there another possible interpretation?)

Did the questioner focus on key ideas or concepts? (What is the main idea you are putting forth? Could you explain that idea?)

Did the questioner note questionable assumptions? (What exactly are you taking for granted here? Why are you assuming that?)

Did the questioner question implications and consequences? (What are you implying when you say...? Are you implying that...? If people accepted your conclusion, and then acted upon it, what implications might follow?)

Did the questioner call attention to the point of view inherent in various answers? (From what point of view are you looking at this? Is there another point of view we should consider?) Did the questioner keep the central question in focus? (I am not sure exactly what question you are raising. Could you explain it? Remember that the question we are dealing with is ...)

Did the questioner call for a clarification of context, when necessary? (Tell us more about the situation that has given rise to this problem. What was going on in this situation?)

Figure 4.8 Socratic questioning (Paul and Elder, 2006).

**Keeping Participants Focused on
Systems For Thought**

Did the questioner distinguish subjective questions from factual questions, from those requiring reasoned judgment within conflicting viewpoints? (Is the question calling for a subjective or personal choice?)

Did the questioner keep the participants aware of alternative ways to think about the problem? (Can you give me another way to think about this problem?)

**Keeping Participants Focused on
Standards For Thought**

Did the questioner call for clarification, when necessary? (Could you elaborate further on what you are saying? Could you give me an example or illustration of your point? Let me tell you what I understand you to be saying. Is my interpretation correct?)

Did the questioner call for more details or greater precision, when necessary? (Could you give us more details about that? Could you specify your allegations more fully?)

Did the questioner keep participants sensitive to the need to check facts and verify the accuracy of information? (How could we check that to see if it is true? How could we verify these alleged facts?)

Did the questioner keep participants aware of the need to stick to the question on the floor; to make sure their "answers" were relevant to the question being addressed at any given point?

Did the questioner keep participants aware of the complexities in the question on the floor? Did the questioner ask participants to think deeply about deep issues?

Figure 4.9 Socratic questioning (continued) (Paul and Elder, 2006).

Simplifying - Revisiting the Space Shuttle Columbia disaster

The Space Shuttle programme was the fourth programme of human spaceflight at the National Aeronautics and Space Administration (NASA), relying on a reusable spacecraft and solid rocket boosters and a disposable external fuel tank. The Space Shuttle could carry up to eight astronauts and a payload of up to 23 tons to a low Earth orbit. The fatal mission of the Columbia was designated STS-107 and was the 113th Space Shuttle launch since the inaugural flight on 12 April 1981 (STS-2).

On 1 February 2003, the Space Shuttle Columbia disintegrated, with the loss of the entire crew. After the 1986 Challenger disaster, it was the second fatal accident in the Space Shuttle programme and considerably tarnished the reputation of NASA.

During the launch of the Space Shuttle Columbia on 16th January, a piece of thermal foam insulation broke off from the external tank and struck reinforced carbon panels on Columbia's left wing. The resulting hole allowed hot gases to enter the wing upon re-entry to Earth's atmosphere.

The Columbia Accident Investigation Board delved into NASA's organisational and cultural shortcomings that led to the accident. A key issue was the excessive pride or self-confidence of NASA in their readiness and preparedness to manage uncertainty:

> The Von Braunean dedication to flawless performance was replaced by an emphasis on efficiency during President Nixon's term in office. At about the same time, NASA also implemented a hierarchical decision structure that separated decision making into levels and accorded substantial power to decision-makers at the top level. Many managers operating in this new arrangement lulled themselves into believing that NASA's early successes were due to the agency's – and perhaps their – invulnerability.
>
> (Mason, 2004, p. 134)

Just-this-way and just-for-now

Despite the Challenger disaster in 1986, repeated successes in launching the Space Shuttle bred complacency and a sense of 'invulnerability'. As it was not the first time thermal foam insulation had broken off the Space Shuttle's external tank, such events became normalised. Over time, these near-miss incidents attracted less and less appraisal, and the perceived need to assess their true value and significance was diminishing. Principally, it became just-this-way of simplifying near-misses to an extent that did not warrant any further scrutiny (see Figure 4.10).

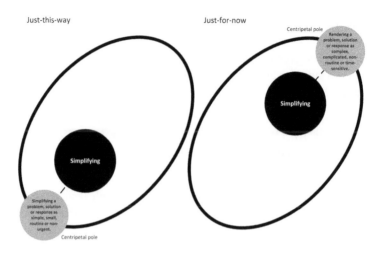

Figure 4.10 Just-this-way and just-for-now polarity (simplifying).

The inference of the opposite pole, just-for-now, would have led NASA to consider every near-miss with the same intensity, assessing its significance repeatedly, and also to question its ability to contain possible ramifications from such an incident, even though in all previous launches, the breaking off of insulation foam had not resulted in a catastrophe. In combination with all other near-misses, the Space Shuttle would never have been allowed to take off, as near-miss after near-miss would have cast doubt on the viability of a launch.

Just-in-case and just-in-time

The world around us is complex; too complex for us to comprehend unless we simplify. We can rely on a plethora of tools, techniques, and practices to simplify the anticipation and response to impending adversity. Unfortunately, by oversimplifying, we create blind spots and miss the crucial details we need to prevent, contain, and recover from adversity (Weick and Sutcliffe, 2006; Langer and Beard, 2014). Consequently, we need a bit of both centripetal and centrifugal force to simplify and scrutinise.

Weighing the pros and cons of the process of simplifying, and the detrimental effects of using either pole, we may come closer to a just-in-case appreciation of both poles (see Figure 4.11). Simplifying is advantageous as it enables us to make sense of adversity in the first place. The reliance on probabilities as a simplifying variable helps us recycle old thoughts or patterns of behaviours (see Chapter 3). Just as centripetal wisdom tells us that ignoring complexity is ill-advised, it is also misguided to overuse the other extreme, characterised by constant, never-ending analysis of different perspectives, interdependencies, and interactions. We may find ourselves paralysed, chasing the ideal but elusive quality of understanding complexity in full as we try to move on.

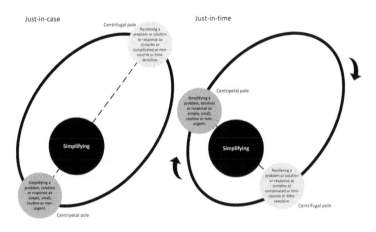

Figure 4.11 Just-in-case and just-in-time polarity (simplifying).

Nevertheless, simplifications in our thought process prevent us from appreciating the complexity of the 'here and now'. They constrain the dynamic, context-based assessment of incidents that we have not yet experienced, that we cannot yet articulate with confidence through probabilistic, root cause assessments.

Simplifying the world around us provides us with a comfortable feeling of dealing with something that is merely complicated and thus manageable. The more we simplify, the more we can break down impending adversity into neat, distinguishable parts that can be managed in isolation from each other. However, by doing this, we may miss crucial details that allow us to stop near-misses and actual incidents triggering a crisis. This leaves us with the question of what is the 'sweet spot' between simplifying and scrutinising:

JUST-IN-CASE, we need to simplify WHILE being reluctant to oversimplify. We may not know what to be vigilant about if we do not know what to look out for. Signals of simplifications are all around us, expressed by us and others, and amplified and locked in as expressions presenting the complex as simple and thus as manageable. It is a challenge to make us sensitive to these signals. As a first step, we may focus on our own communication and writings and highlight possible simplifications. Then we could add others to provide us with a constructive challenge to the simplifications we may have identified.

JUST-IN-CASE, we prefer to reduce stakeholder ambiguity WHILE updating expectations. Chapters 2 and 3 have reinforced the need to consider multiple perspectives and the appreciation of complexity. Not only may these different perspectives be in conflict with each other but they may also reveal commonalities and interactive dependencies. To ignore them for the sake of representing something that is complex as if it were simple is ill-advised:

> Fresh eyes tend to break up the mind-set that perpetuates fixation. When people resist simplification, they tend to break up fixations. Your job is to be sure that people keep updating as evidence changes.

> (Weick and Sutcliffe, 2015, p. 76)

JUST-IN-CASE, we seek to simplify WHILE doubting our assumptions. Engaging, for example, with Socratic questioning, appreciating that there is no single answer to a problem, may not go down well, as it prevents us from moving on with our decision-making. Moreover, it may confuse, baffle, disorient, and thus frustrate us. So, the scene must be set, and communication must be shaped (see Chapter 8) to enable us to question and challenge our propensity to oversimplify.

The integration of both poles, as indicated by the previously stated principles, provides a third way of managing the unexpected. Sitting between the two poles – simplifying a problem, solution, or response as simple, small, routine, or non-urgent and the opposite pole of rendering a problem, solution, or response as complex or complicated, non-routine, or time-sensitive – could enable managing the unexpected to be shaped by another process: communicating (see Chapter 8). However, to move to just-in-time paradoxical thinking, we need to be ready, just-in-time, to reconfigure the balance of gravitational forces in real-time, by adding a condition that defines how long we adhere to the initially defined just-in-case principles. The first just-in-case principle could be expanded to the following just-in-time rule by adding a temporal condition:

We need to simplify WHILE being reluctant to oversimplify AS LONG AS we share information extensively, transparently, or openly.

The extent to which we share information extensively, transparently, or openly (see Chapter 8) regulates our temptation to oversimplify. With more information freely shared, there are more opportunities to pay attention to the clues that help us to examine a problem, solution, or response with greater scrutiny.

Towards a paradox mindset

As in the previous chapters, we should be reluctant to give in to either/or thinking; we should refuse to abandon centripetal wisdom and nor should we replace it with opposite just-for-now ideas of managing adversity. In any case, probabilistic risk management and root cause analyses are here to stay, and with reason. Nonetheless, by acknowledging and embracing some opposing wisdom, we may reconceptualise reductionist, probabilistic, and root-cause-based assessments and expand our thinking beyond statistical oversimplifications:

> … risk management can involve a far more subtle and nuanced analytical approach that is often presented in formal models of risk analysis, that typically focuses on predicting the extent of future harm. In practice, risks may be defined and assessed in ways that both extend and contradict current normative models of risk management.

(Macrae, 2009, p. 115)

Ultimately, further paradoxical tensions emerge and challenge our thinking around such tools and techniques when we apply them and see or feel them working out in practice, just-in-time.

References

Bice, M. and Hayes, J. (2009) 'Risk management: From hazard logs to bow-ties', in Hopkins, A. (ed.) *Learning from high reliability organisations*. North Ryde: CHH Australia Limited, pp. 59–85.

Hayes, J. (2009) 'Incident reporting: A nuclear industry case study', in Hopkins, A. (ed.) *Learning from high reliability organisations*. North Ryde: CCH Australia, pp. 117–134.

Hoffman, B. (2017) *Red teaming: Transform your business by thinking like the enemy*. London: Piatkus.

Hopkins, A. (2009) 'Identifying and responding to warnings', in Hopkins, A. (ed.) *Learning from high reliability organisations*. North Ryde: CCH Australia, pp. 33–58.

Juran, J. M. and De Feo, J. A. (2010) *Juran's quality handbook: The complete guide to performance excellence*. New York: McGraw-Hill Education.

Kahneman, D. and Tversky, A. (1972) 'Subjective probability: A judgment of representativeness', *Cognitive Psychology*, 3(3), pp. 430–454.

Langer, E. and Beard, A. (2014) 'Mindfulness in the age of complexity', *Harvard Business Review*, 92(3), pp. 68–73.

Macrae, C. (2009) 'From risk to resilience: Assessing flight safety incidents in airlines', in Hopkins, A. (ed.) *Learning from high reliability organisations*. North Ryde: CCH Australia, pp. 95–115.

Mason, R. O. (2004) 'Lessons in organizational ethics from the Columbia disaster: Can a culture be lethal?', *Organizational Dynamics*, 33(2), pp. 128–142.

Paul, R. and Elder, L. (2006) 'Socratic questioning', in *The thinker's guide to the art of socratic questioning*. Foundation for Critical Thinking, pp. 1–90.

Ready, D. A. (2002) 'How storytelling builds next-generation leaders', *MIT Sloan Management Review*, 43(4), pp. 63–70.

Weick, K. and Sutcliffe, K. (2001) *Managing the unexpected: Assuring high performance in an age of complexity*. San Francisco, CA: Jossey Bass.

Weick, K. and Sutcliffe, K. (2006) 'Mindfulness and the quality of organizational attention', *Organization Science*, 17(4), pp. 514–524.

Weick, K. and Sutcliffe, K. (2007) *Managing the unexpected: Resilient performance in an age of uncertainty*. 2nd edn. San Francisco, CA: Jossey Bass.

Weick, K. and Sutcliffe, K. (2015) *Managing the unexpected: Sustained performance in a complex world*. 3rd edn. Hoboken, NJ: Wiley.

Chapter 5

Following procedures, processes, or policies

A persistent challenge in high-reliability management is deciding whether to follow a path rigidly or constantly change direction (see Figure 5.1). In other words, we are struggling to break free from norms, routines, and the authoritative power of orders, rules, processes, and front-loaded best practice frameworks.

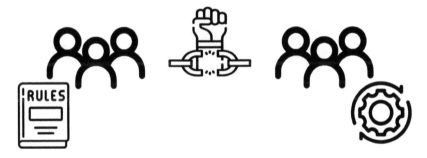

Figure 5.1 Freedom to act.

The freedom to act is the opposite of being slavishly obedient to rules, processes, a higher authority, or our own impulses. Having authority over our own doing is, however, challenging:

> When we make decisions, we're not always in charge. We can be too impulsive or too deliberate for our own good; one moment we hot-headedly let our emotions get the better of us, and the next we're paralysed by uncertainty. Then we'll pull a brilliant decision out of thin air – and wonder how we did it.

> (Morse, 2006, p. 42)

Although following procedures, processes, policies, routines, and habits is unsurprisingly centripetal wisdom (see Figure 5.2), we are also provided with an opposite choice of ignoring the very same procedures, delaying them, or innovating a response if we believe that existing procedures, processes, and policies do not serve as well in anticipating and containing impending adversity.

87

DOI: 10.4324/9781003083115-5

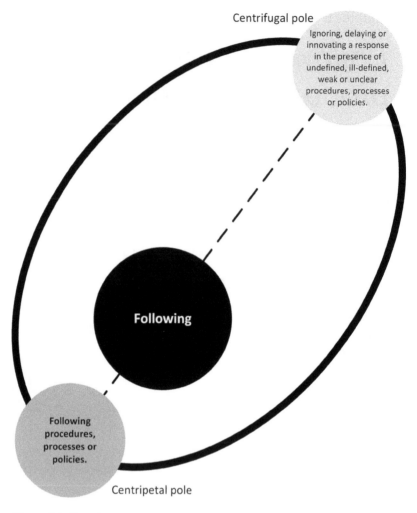

Centrifugal pole

Ignoring, delaying or
innovating a response
in the presence of
undefined, ill-defined,
weak or unclear
procedures, processes
or policies.

Following

Following
procedures,
processes or
policies.

Centripetal pole

Figure 5.2 Centripetal and centrifugal forces (following).

Centripetal wisdom

Our freedom to act, not just follow somebody else's lead, or an order, a process, a rule, or a task, sets us apart from those who are less capable of being mindful. And yet, in the face of impending adversity, our longing for latitude in determining what we want and what we need to do is constrained by some of the following biases and inclinations:

Conformity. The conformity bias is an inclination to match beliefs and behaviours to norms that are shared by other people instead of using our own judgement

(Moscovici and Faucheux, 1972). In other words, we tend to follow the herd, mimicking other people or society's norms.

Proficiency. Compliance with rules, processes, laws, and regulations is supposed to guide decision-making and streamline internal processes. The same process of compliance may reinforce an illusion of control (Langer, 1975) while in fact, responsibility is cast off and transferred to a process or a rule.

Automation. A rulebook is often embedded in electronic decision support systems that provide us with automated assistance in being compliant. The automation bias (Parasuraman and Manzey, 2010) results in complacency, a feeling of contentment with the decision support systems' output. Over time, we allow systems, signifying processes, rules, and regulations, to make decisions for us.

Fixation. The tools, techniques, or instruments that we are compliant with may become familiar, if not too familiar. In this respect, the famous refrain of *"if all you have is a hammer, everything looks like a nail"* (adopted from Maslow, 1966) rings true. Compliance may drive an overreliance on tools, techniques, or instruments, and their outputs.

Not only do our biases make us routinise our actions and essentially reduce our freedom to engage with impending adversity mindfully but the pressure from the external environment also drives an expectation of greater consistency in action. In the wake of incidents, we tend to tighten the screws by imposing more procedures and more rules to reduce situated cognition as a source of error. In other words, we do not think on our feet, as this may cause a problem or incident, or trigger a crisis. Instead, we box in our thinking by reverting to compliance and conformity.

Compliance is defined as the process of following a procedure, process, or policy, and adherence to rulebooks, regimens, and managerial directions set out by regulatory bodies (see Figure 5.3).

Who has not taken part, sometimes reluctantly, in some form of compliance training; perhaps regarding workplace safety, information security, or trade compliance? These are all carried out by organisations to uphold their regimens. In combination, our urge to routinise our actions and the promotion of compliant behaviour result in habit-based, unchanging and mechanically performed activities, practices, and actions.

The resulting compliance culture is reinforced by consistent messaging about the expected compliance's nature, breadth, and depth. Activities, actions, and practices are monitored through predefined performance measures, often in the form of audits. Any violations of the compliance regime will result in punitive action and adherence to it in rewards.

Figure 5.3 Compliance in collective decision-making.

A compliance culture in an organisation produces a range of benefits. It fosters clarity in action in that it provides employees with an unambiguous and undisputed course of action. This allows a quick auto-pilot activation of activity, devoid of the need for situational analysis of the context in which this action is carried out. Last but not least, a compliant organisation or work unit forms the foundation for legal accountability.

The toolbox

The checklist. A checklist is a standardised list of steps to take, usually reserved for repetitive tasks (see Figure 5.4). With checklists, the management of near-misses and accidents is front-loaded; they aim to help us get organised and not forget any important steps:

> Here, then, is our situation at the start of the twenty-first century: We have accumulated stupendous know-how. We have put it in the hands of some of the most highly trained, highly skilled, and hardworking people in our society. And with it, they have accomplished extraordinary things. Nonetheless, that know-how is often unmanageable. Avoidable failures are common and persistent, not to mention demoralising and frustrating, across many fields – from medicine to finance, business to government. And the reason is increasingly evident: the volume and complexity of what we know has exceeded our individual ability to deliver its benefits correctly, safely, or reliably. Knowledge has both saved us and burdened us. That means we need a different strategy

for overcoming failure, one that builds on experience and takes advantage of the knowledge people have but somehow also makes up for our human inadequacies. And there is such a strategy – though it will seem almost ridiculous in its simplicity, maybe even crazy to those of us who have spent years carefully developing ever more advanced skills and technologies. It is a checklist.

(Gawande, 2010, p. 13)

Figure 5.4 Checklist.

A checklist is slightly different to a procedure or policy. A checklist tends to focus only on what to do and at times it also indicates who should do it. The main purpose of a checklist is to ensure that tasks are completed quickly and efficiently.

Risk control. For a third time (see Chapters 3 and 4), we will look at probabilistic risk management; however, with reference to the construct of the following, only the aspect of risk control (see Figure 5.5) will be scrutinised in more detail.

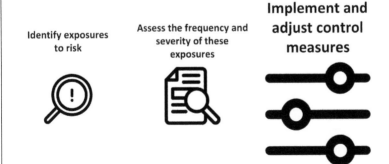

Figure 5.5 Risk control.

Risk control measures may include the

- elimination of risk (by, for example, de-scoping the problem)

- substitution of risk with a lesser risk

- reduction in the likelihood of occurrence

- mitigation of potential impact

- modification of the environment (so that the risk is less likely to materialise or will materialise less quickly)

- establishment of safeguards

- development of procedural methods (e.g. safer ways of operating)

- protection of critical assets and functions (in case a risk materialises)

Stifling-situated cognition

The dark side of a compliance culture, augmented by checklists and risk controls, is that it constrains situated cognition. The organisational regimen front-loads our actions; we routinise our behaviours, practices, and actions mindlessly, without evaluating context. This, in turn, predisposes our view of near-misses and accidents. If this predisposition is confronted with novelty, we are likely to feel unprepared for it. Ultimately, we run on autopilot.

> Despite all the rhetoric and money invested in it, risk management is often treated as a compliance issue that can be solved by drawing up lots of rules and making sure that all employees follow them. Many such rules, of course, are sensible and do reduce some risks that could severely damage a company. But rules-based risk management will not diminish the likelihood or the impact of a disaster such as Deepwater Horizon, just as it did not prevent the failure of many financial institutions during the 2007–2008 credit crisis.

> (Kaplan and Mikes, 2012, p. 50)

Self-serving

We tend to be rewarded if we are compliant and punished when not. Consequently, it is tempting to comply and conform for the sake of furthering our own interests, rather than those of the work unit on whose behalf we are managing adversity.

Self-evidently correct

The imposition of a regimen of rules drives the practice of self-evidently correct routines, which do not require proof or explanation. We follow them for the sake of being compliant, even if the routine may seem absurd to us.

Lack of sensitivity

Just as we conform to routines because they are in our (self-serving) interests and do not require any validation, we also tend to rely on individual habits in isolation of each other, being unaware of their impact on the problem at hand, as well as on each other. Once we have adhered to a rule or process and completed a routine, as expected of us, we move to the next in a Taylorist (Taylor, 1911) manner, devoid of sensitivity to the consequences of our auto-pilot behaviour.

Anonymity and authority

The mere requirement to be compliant may make us feel like a 'cog in the wheel'. The authority of compliance diminishes the perceived importance of our situated cognition as a means of preventing and containing adversity. In essence, we just need to 'tick the box', and so the process, rule, or routine deauthorises our longing to think.

 ## Centrifugal wisdom

The limitations in driving collective decision-making through compliance with control systems are summarised by Hamel (2009, p. 93):

> Traditional control systems ensure high levels of compliance but do so at the expense of employee creativity, entrepreneurship, and engagement. To overcome the discipline-versus-innovation trade-off, tomorrow's control systems will need to rely more on peer review and less on top-down

supervision. They must leverage the power of shared values and aspirations while loosening the straitjacket of rules and strictures. The goal: organisations filled with employees who are capable of self-discipline.

Hence, relying on compliance is questionable because of the front-loading of past-informed processes, rules, and procedures that are to be applied in a mindless but disciplined, efficient manner, despite being ill-equipped to activate a response to novel problems the pre-configured rulebook does not have an answer to.

Rationalist, top-down, and front-loaded actions are still a tempting proposition for organisations. To reduce situated cognition as a source of error, we tend to break down our past experiences into smaller, controllable actions to which we adhere; any rule-breaking will result in punitive measures; and rule-following will be rewarded. The codification of common problems drives the routinisation of behaviours and actions, thus contributing to an ever-growing repository of best practices that we can rely on mindlessly.

In an HRO, the prevailing mantra is less one of routines and more one of the mindful appropriation of rules, processes, procedures, and routine practices:

> When considering how safety rules are tools, the focus is not on how members follow rules, nor on how rules dictate action (as with the rationalist approach). Instead, the focus is on how members appropriate safety rules – how they draw from safety rules to access lessons from catastrophes, and how they use safety rules to make present or visible organisational priorities and lessons.
>
> (Jahn, 2016, p. 366)

Discretion and commitment

Good judgement involves the appropriation of rules and routines. Hence, discretion implies the freedom to define, deviate, adapt, and make decisions that reside outside the formalised front-loading of behaviours and actions.

In contrast to an external commitment (see Table 5.1), defined as contractual compliance, the discretion to act is a participative process (Argyris, 1998) that allows us, individuals, to appropriate rules, routines, and practices.

The discretion to act, through internal commitment, tends to foster greater job satisfaction, as we feel less like an externally operated 'cog in the wheel' and more like an individual creator of rules and routines.

Table 5.1 External versus Internal Commitment

How Commitment Differs

External Commitment	Internal Commitment
Tasks are defined by others	Individuals define tasks
The behaviour required to perform tasks is defined by others	Individuals define the behaviour required to perform tasks
Performance goals are defined by management	Management and individuals jointly define performance goals and values that are challenging for the individuals
The importance of the goal is defined by others	Individuals define the importance of goals and values

Source: Adopted from Argyris, 1998, p. 100.

Value-driven appropriation

The discretionary management that we may internally commit ourselves to does not provide us with a carte-blanche, a free-for-all style of managing adversity. A value-based mindset (Ginsburg and Miller, 1992) can be best understood as guiding and directing behaviours and decision-making towards commonly shared values. Hence, the appropriation of rules and routines is driven, and constrained, by the extent to which values such as profitability, integrity, quality, or productivity are supported.

Expertise

The need for us to appropriate rules, routines, and habits as a means of creating novel responses to impending incidents requires an abundance of expertise and the willingness to have such expertise challenged.

The build-up of expertise requires investment in people, in the form of training and learning exercises. A valuable expertise-building approach is the provision of stretch assignments (Douglas and Jay, 2007, see also toolbox). These may take the form of giving us a project or task that is beyond our current knowledge or skills level.

Sensitivity

Value-driven appropriation of rules and routines imposes limits on the extent to which we internally commit ourselves to deviate from an established regimen. Within these limits, we need to be keenly aware of the consequences of actions; we need to stay attentive to the ramifications of our discretion to appropriate rules and routines. Such sensitivity is fostered through frequent interaction and familiarity with each other's jobs (Weick and Sutcliffe, 2015). Subsequently, we each constantly align our respective discretion regarding rule appropriation with others, addressing emerging tensions of interoperability.

Mindful training

Under the umbrella of centripetal wisdom, we may be trained to front-load our actions, to drill them into ourselves, so we can repeat them efficiently. As beneficial as such training would be in rendering our management of adversity automatic, it is nevertheless detrimental in the context of any novelty we might face. As a consequence, the centrifugal definition of training is one of thinking and acting beyond the mechanics of a checklist or risk controls:

> The lessons learned are simple: organisations that have fewer accidents are those that teach their people how to recognise and respond to a variety of problems and empower them to act. The training teaches people not only how to react to specific situations, but also, and perhaps more importantly, how to respond to situations that aren't in the training manual. Preventive training also includes recognising decoys or false trails, so that people see that not everything is as it appears. Finally, such training helps people recognise how to decouple highly coupled systems quickly to minimise the harm caused by the initial accident to the total system.
>
> (Roberts and Bea, 2001, p. 73)

Trust and recognition

Rule-based and routine appropriations require an atmosphere of trust in which people are not automatically labelled and scrutinised as rule benders or breakers. Indeed, we must be trusted to appropriate rules and routines with integrity and with a clear commitment to realise those values that are important to the organisation. This does not imply that if bad behaviour (e.g. gross negligence) is observed, it will not result in punitive actions (Reason, 1997). Nevertheless, if we apply our discretionary power to appropriate rules and routines in a value-adding manner, then we should be incentivised and rewarded.

The toolbox

Stretch assignments. The successful appropriation of rules and routines
does not come out of thin air. In acquiring and honing such skills, stretch
assignments serve as valuable opportunities to develop adaptive expertise.
Stretch assignments tend to require us to accomplish a task or a project
for which answers have not yet been defined or solutions have not developed. Thus a stretch assignment takes us out of our rule/routine zone
(see Figure 5.6);the task or the project does not reflect routine work but
is unfamiliar and uncomfortable to us.

The coordination of stretch assignments (see Figure 5.6) requires the definition of checkpoints to allow us to take stock of how far we have moved
beyond our own, hardwired mental schema of rules and routines. If they are
embedded in the routine work of our organisation, touchpoints with the rule/
routine zones, as well as the opposite extreme, the inappropriateness zone,
need to be carefully monitored. Such monitoring and provision of interim
feedback may be carried out by a mentor who is emotionally and structurally detached from the mentee, to allow objective and impersonal feedback.

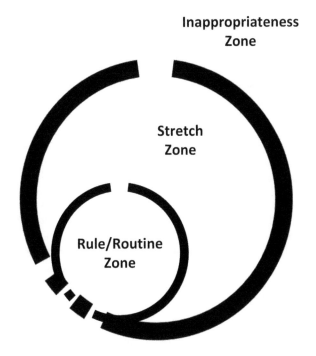

Figure 5.6 Zones of rule/routine appropriation.

Improvisation. The process of 'in-the-moment' appropriation of rules and routines (see Figure 5.7) builds on the key skills of improvisation:

> In general terms, improvisation is the ability to create and implement a new or unplanned solution in the face of an unexpected problem or change. It is often seen as spontaneous, intuitive, creative problem-solving behaviour that happens 'mostly on the fly'.
>
> (Conforto, Rebentisch, and Amaral, 2016, p. 8)

Within the boundaries of the positively shaped (see Figure 5.6) stretch zone, improvisation thrives. This may include the temporary or permanent empowerment for us to make a mindful, in-the-moment decision, while nevertheless informed by expertise and with awareness of the inappropriateness zone. Furthermore, open, frequent day-to-day communication with mentors and outside experts provides objective feedback on the improvisational activities of the team.

Build a culture that recognises and views change positively	Create the right team structure and project environment	Provide management practices and tools that facilitate improvisation

Figure 5.7 Fostering business improvisation (adapted from Conforto, Rebentisch and Amaral, 2016).

To help us define and sharpen our improvisation skills, we will draw on the fields of arts (White, 2021) and entertainment, where improvisation is considered a vital skill. Below are three simple to carry-out improvisation exercises used in comedy (extracted from Yorton, 2022):

Embrace the ensemble. Gather five to ten people in a circle and create a new story, with each person, in turn, contributing a single word. Go around a dozen times, then stop to check-in. Participants quickly learn that they have to balance their own ideas and expectations with those of the ensemble. No one can control the outcome. And words like 'the' or 'and' are just as important as 'tortoise' or 'hare'. Seemingly small contributions matter greatly to the whole.

Take responsible risk. Two people engage in a conversation about anything, but have to begin every sentence with the words, 'thank you'. This underscores a key idea in improv: everything your colleagues offer is a gift about which you should feel grateful. When comedians, or leaders, create an environment that welcomes and values contributions, people are willing to give bolder, more honest comments and take more risks.

Follow the follower. A group makes a circle; one person stands in the middle, eyes closed. Everyone else silently chooses one member of the circle to be the leader and then begins to mimic the movements the leader makes. The person in the middle opens his or her eyes and tries to determine who the leader is. We use this exercise to reinforce the idea that high-functioning improv ensembles find their leaders by looking for the right person at the right time, not formal titles.

Following - Revisiting the Chernobyl disaster

After World War II, the former USSR invested heavily in nuclear power. By the end of 1985, it had a total capacity of 1,500 billion kilowatt-hours, covering 14% of the electricity needed. Most of the power plants in the 1980s were boiling-water, high-power reactors (in short, RBMK-1000). One of them was the Vladimir Lenin Nuclear Power Plant, located near the city of Pripyat (close to the border with Belarus) in the Ukrainian Soviet Socialist Republic.

On 25th April 1986, routine maintenance was scheduled in reactor 4; this included carrying out a safety test that mimics a power loss; if a power plant loses power, the reactor still needs to be cooled. In 1982, 1984, and 1985, such tests were conducted, but all yielded negative results. Another test was scheduled, initially to be carried out by the day shift. Nevertheless, because another power station went offline in the Kiev region, that test was postponed and overseen by a comparatively inexperienced evening shift.

The first step was to decrease the power to 700 megawatts (MW) at midnight on 25 April. In fact, the power collapsed to a near-shutdown stage at 30 MW. Despite this oddity, the operators increased output to 200 MW, still far below the 700 MW outlined in the test protocol. The test officially began at 1:23:04 AM on 26 April. Unbeknown to the operators, due to the near stall of the reactor, the core became unstable, and the final steps resulted in a power outage that was not contained by an emergency shutdown, but because of the design of the reactor, the sudden emergency shutdown fuelled a jump in output to an unsustainable 30,000 MW. At 1:23:58 AM, reactor 4 of the Vladimir Lenin Nuclear Power Plant exploded. It is widely considered the worst power plant accident in history.

A multitude of causes has been identified to explain this disaster. In addition to the design deficiencies in all RMBK reactors, another aspect was the inexperience of the evening shift and their adherence to a test protocol that they followed almost religiously under unsafe conditions:

> Immediately upon the start of the shift, Diatlov began demanding that the program continue to be carried out. When Akimov sat down to study the program, Diatlov began reproaching him for working too slowly and failing to pay attention to the complexity of the situation that had arisen in the unit. Diatlov shouted at Akimov to get up and started insisting that he hurry up. Akimov, holding a sheaf of papers in his hands (evidently the program), began going around to the control room operators and establishing whether the equipment was in appropriate condition for the program that was being carried out.
>
> (Plokhy, 2018, pp. 79–80)

Just-this-way and just-for-now

Centripetal wisdom may dictate that following processes, procedures, and policies is the only legitimate way to avert adversity. The biases we have may amplify the propensity to routinise our practices, so in essence, we are tempted to run on autopilot. It requires less effort; it is efficient; and accountability for our actions can be deflected away from us, and instead directed at the front-loaded autopilot.

Over the years, operators and engineers became more accustomed to the new technology of an RBMK reactor. Guidelines, manuals, checklists, and procedures were produced for running a reactor; they were refined and matured to allow safe operation, although safety was often compromised in order to meet productivity targets. The just-this-way management of adversity (see Figure 5.8) is, unsurprisingly, one of strict compliance, fortified at times by an excessive notion of obedience to a higher authority.

Let's assume the opposite just-for-now pole is centripetal to our argument of anticipating and containing near-misses and accidents. This would imply that operators question manuals and processes; even their experience and routines will need to be examined whenever they run a power plant. Even when faced with low-hazard tasks or tasks that do not immediately affect critical function, these would have to be continuously scrutinised. This extreme polar opposite of following procedures, processes or policies seems as nonsensical as strict conformity to automated, compliance-based management of adversity.

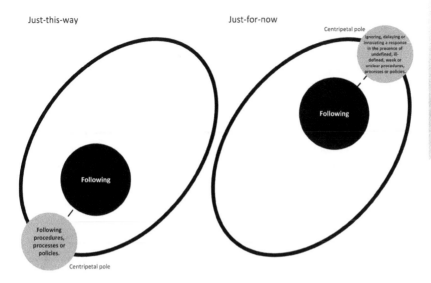

Figure 5.8 Just-this-way and just-for-now polarity (following).

The discourse on just-this-way and the opposite just-for-now has been widely covered in academic literature. To quote just one contribution on the pros and cons of being compliant:

> On the one hand, the traditional view assumes that the increasing standardisation of individual, group and organisational behaviours leads to higher predictability of safe outcomes. Therefore, managers have defended the adoption of strict compliance based on the argument that if procedures or rules are not strictly followed, workers could easily fall into deviant practices that can lead to catastrophic consequences. On the other hand, according to recent research, safety compliance alone is not sufficient to ensure the best possible safety levels, and it has even been considered dangerous under certain special or unexpected circumstances. This perspective argues that any complex system susceptible to unpredictability and uncertainty should accept 'necessary deviations' or 'make adjustments' to the rules and procedures in order to manage a given situation while being as resilient as possible.
>
> (Martínez-Córcoles *et al.*, 2014, p. 1258)

Just-in-case and just-in-time

As we are creatures of habit, we are tempted to routinise experiences. It is commonplace to think that rigid adherence to rules and routines is the one best way of anticipating and responding to near-miss and actual incidents. We reason that it reduces our fallibilities and the possibilities for us to make mistakes. So we automatise our actions; we are made and conditioned to switch to an autopilot mentality, being compliant with a regiment of front-loaded decisions and actions. Essentially, conforming and complying is effortless, straightforward, and uncomplicated; it is more efficient.

The opposite pole to strict compliance and conformity is one of improvisation and stretching our thinking beyond norms, authority, and status. Here, we may come up with solutions the rulebook does not provide. We create novel solutions to the novel problems signified by near-misses and accidents, although the activity of improvising is not sustainable in the long run.

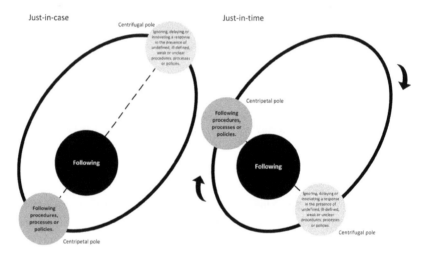

Figure 5.9 Just-in-case and just-in-time polarity (following).

Although this chapter started with the centripetal wisdom of compliance to a regimen of rules, procedures, and rules, it is reasonable to assume that we need both centripetal and centrifugal wisdom to be integrated into a third option, a less polarised set of just-in-case (see Figure 5.9) principles:

JUST-IN-CASE, we are compelled to adhere to an organisational regime WHILE appropriating and creating new rules, routines, procedures, and policies. In every organisation, there certainly will be a regimen, a regulated system that we may have to obey, although hopefully not in a slavish manner. That is not to suggest that we should join an organisation with the intention of being a rule bender and breaker. Still, a culture that fosters mindful rule appropriation provides us with 'wriggle room' to continuously challenge, define, and adapt our actions to the environmental challenges we face – within limits. Ergo, we need to recognise the existence of top-down rules (Argyris 1998) while exploiting the limited adaptive space we are given.

JUST-IN-CASE, we defer to authority, rank, and status WHILE assuming power to deviate from rules, routines, procedures, and policies. Within the stretch zone, we empower each other and take power and authority to prevent or contain the consequences of an incident. The process of supporting each other or claiming power by ourselves needs to be value-adding, though. This requires us to understand the ramifications of our actions and the boundaries of inappropriateness, which limit the extent of rule and routine appropriation. We need to understand what we want to do while always being mindful of what we must not do!

JUST-IN-CASE, we commit ourselves to an organisational regimen WHILE stretching our thinking beyond it. Operating in a stretch zone, applying in-the-moment skills such as improvisation, may quickly end up as a daunting, overwhelming, and ultimately chaotic experience. Mentoring can re-establish some form of structure through active listening, reflecting, clarifying, coaching, and providing constructive feedback. Mentoring can make us understand the breadth and depth of the choices we have in a stretch zone; it helps us learn in which situations it is best to adhere to a rule or routine and when not to.

JUST-IN-CASE, we tick off a checklist for repetitive tasks WHILE being mindful of impending adversity to which we have no prescribed answer. This principle means that our primary approach to managing adversity is one of being 'on autopilot' that enables us to deal with repetitive tasks which are not critical to the functioning of operations or to performance. While routine-like reliability defines our management of near-misses and accidents, we also put aside time, effort and space to create new routines, rules, procedures, and policies, in real-time:

> The first time you go through a checklist, it's fine. But after that, most people tend to do it mindlessly. So in aviation you have flaps up, throttle open, anti-ice off. But if snow is coming and the anti-ice is off, the plane crashes.
>
> Checklists aren't bad if they require qualitative information to be obtained in that moment. For example, 'Please note the weather conditions. Based on these conditions, should the anti-ice be on or off?' or 'How is the patient's skin color different from yesterday?' If you ask questions that encourage mindfulness, you bring people into the present and you're more likely to avoid an accident.
>
> (Langer and Beard, 2014, p. 72)

The just-in-case integration of both centripetal and centrifugal poles of the construct of the following seems reasonable. Still, the third option that results from such integration must not remain static in its configuration. Just-in-time, these principles require a timestamp that sets boundaries on time. To take only the first just-in-case principle, that might be expanded as follows:

JUST-IN-TIME, we are compelled to adhere to an organisational regimen WHILE appropriating and creating new rules, routines, procedures, and policies AS LONG AS we are sensitive about the consequences of our actions. As long as we have established, maintained, and updated a bigger picture than the one we are sensitive about (see Chapter 7), we understand the ramifications of our actions. If that bigger picture is lost, incomprehensible or too ambiguous (see Chapter 2), the management of incidents should be delayed until the bigger picture has been re-established.

Towards a paradox mindset

Centripetal wisdom may dictate that following processes, procedures, and policies is the only legitimate way to avert adversity. The biases we face may amplify the propensity to routinise our practices. In essence, we are tempted to run on autopilot, meaning that we do what we are expected to do and are programmed for certain behaviours and actions without any real, conscious, and mindful involvement. That requires less effort; it is efficient; and accountability for action can be deflected away from us and instead towards the front-loaded autopilot.

And yet, as absurd as it is for an autopilot mentality to be put forward as a universal solution, it is equally absurd to see the extreme opposite idea of continuously stretching our minds and actions as occupying that role through improvisation and operating beyond the realm of routines, rules, processes, and policies.

As a consequence, your high-reliability management of near-misses and accidents may well be defined by warring principles that are paradoxical and yet beneficial, not set in stone but constantly challenged, questioned, elaborated, and evaluated, in case you need them, just-in-time.

References

Argyris, C. (1998) 'Empowerment: The emperor's new clothes', *Harvard Business Review*, 76(3), pp. 98–105.

Conforto, E. C., Rebentisch, E. and Amaral, D. (2016) 'Learning the art of business improvisation', *MIT Sloan Management Review*, 57(3), pp. 8–10.

Douglas, A. R. and Jay, A. C. (2007) 'Make your company a talent factory', *Harvard Business Review*, 85(6), pp. 68–77.

Gawande, A. (2010) *Checklist manifesto*. London: Profile Books.

Ginsburg, L. and Miller, N. (1992) 'Value-driven management.', *Business Horizons*, 35(3), p. 23.

Hamel, G. (2009) 'Moon shots for management', *Harvard Business Review*, 87(6), pp. 91–98.

Jahn, J. L. S. (2016) 'Adapting safety rules in a high reliability context', *Management Communication Quarterly*, 30(3), pp. 362–389.

Kaplan, R. and Mikes, A. (2012) 'Managing risks: A new framework', *Harvard Business Review*, 90(6), pp. 48–60.

Langer, E. and Beard, A. (2014) 'Mindfulness in the age of complexity', *Harvard Business Review*, 92(3), pp. 68–73.

Langer, E. J. (1975) 'The illusion of control', *Journal of Personality and Social Psychology*, 32(2), pp. 311–328.

Martínez-Córcoles, M. *et al.* (2014) 'Strengthening safety compliance in nuclear power operations: A role-based approach', *Risk Analysis*, 34(7), pp. 1257–1269.

Maslow, A. H. (1966) *The psychology of science; A reconnaissance.* New York: Harper & Row.

Morse, G. (2006) 'Decisions and desire', *Harvard Business Review*, 84(1), pp. 42–51.

Moscovici, S., & Faucheux, C. (1972). Social influence, conformity bias, and the study of active minorities. *Advances in Experimental Social Psychology*, 6(C), 149–202

Parasuraman, R. and Manzey, D. H. (2010) 'Complacency and bias in human use of auto- mation: An attentional integration', *Human Factors*, 52(3), pp. 381–410.

Plokhy, S. (2018) *Chernobyl: History of a tragedy.* London: Penguin Books Limited.

Reason, J. (1997) *Managing the risks of organisational accidents.* Aldershot: Ashgate.

Roberts, K. H. and Bea, R. (2001) 'Must accidents happen? Lessons from high reliability organizations', *The Academy of Management Executive*, 15(3), pp. 70–79.

Taylor, F. W. (1911) *The principles of scientific management.* New York: Harper Brothers.

Weick, K. and Sutcliffe, K. (2015) *Managing the unexpected: Sustained performance in a complex world.* 3rd edn. Hoboken, NJ: Wiley.

White, K. (2021). *Use Art to Reignite Your Team's Motivation.* Harvard Business Review. https://hbr.org/2021/03/use-art-to-reignite-your-teams-motivation

Yorton, T. (2022) *3 Improv Exercises That Can Change the Way Your Team Works.* Harvard Business Review. https://hbr.org/2015/03/3-improv-exercises-that-can- change-the-way-your-team-works

Chapter 6

Influencing responses, actions, or solutions

The term management may be defined as exercising influence or having control over adversity. Even so, the idea of exercising a dominating influence over our environment is constantly challenged:

> ... control can be lost by not being ready to respond, by having too little time, by lacking knowledge of what is going on, or by lacking the necessary resources. To maintain control unsurprisingly requires the converse of these conditions.

(Masys, 2015, p. vii)

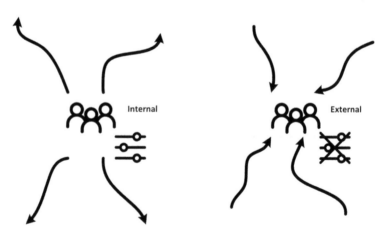

Figure 6.1 Internal and external locus of control.

On one hand, when something is about to go wrong, we may blame ourselves for not preventing a near-miss or actual incident from snowballing into a crisis. On the other, we might attribute our ability to control, and our lack of control, to the external environment (see Figure 6.1). In essence, we believe that either we make things happen or things are happening to us:

106

DOI: 10.4324/9781003083115-6

A locus of control orientation is a belief about whether the outcomes of our actions are contingent on what we do (internal control orientation) or on events outside our personal control (external control orientation).

(Saha, 2006, p. 213)

Locus of control provides us with a sense of agency in regard to our ability to exert influence. In the context of preventing adversity, it defines the extent to which we believe we can anticipate and respond to near-miss and actual incidents; our aptitude for doing so is very much dependent on our locus of control.

Exercising a strong influence over near-misses and accidents as a means to prevent a crisis from materialising is an additional construct that we deem salient. As illustrated in Figure 6.2, the bipolarity we face lies within instead of outside our ability to influence.

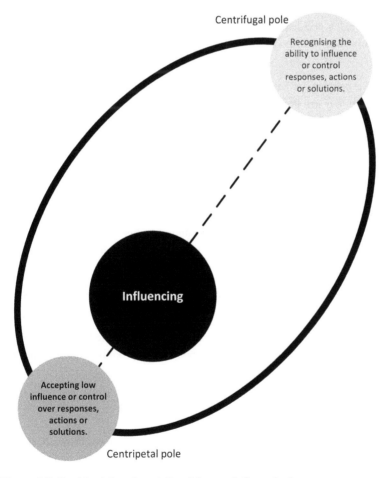

Centrifugal pole

Recognising the ability to influence or control responses, actions or solutions.

Influencing

Accepting low influence or control over responses, actions or solutions.

Centripetal pole

Figure 6.2 Centripetal and centrifugal forces (influencing).

To facilitate an early response to both types of incidents, we should widen the sphere of our ability to influence the management of looming adversity by also acknowledging our shortcomings and limitations in controlling adversity.

 ## Centripetal wisdom

When we are faced with the possibility of impending adversity derailing our set objectives, aims, and outcomes, we may initially engage with it with an illusory belief in our ability to avert any adversity. However, by default, this illusion is constantly challenged by managerial imperfections, so that the initial internal locus of control is quickly converted into pessimism and hopelessness:

Fatalism. You may have noticed that, in the previous chapters, we focussed on optimism and egotistical self-confidence in determining our management of adversity. Fatalism is the opposite of that; it may be likened to a feeling of events being decided by fate; they are fixed in advance, inevitable, and outside our influence:

> … people who have fatalist beliefs may think that there is little or nothing that they can do to avoid or protect themselves from risk and that the locus of control over life events is external to themselves.

> (Liu and Sun, 2021, p. 2)

In this aspect, we may feel powerless; no matter what we do, the future is already predetermined. A fatalistic tendency may be amplified by some of the previously mentioned construct poles. We may feel powerless as we are obliged to follow rules and procedures. Conformity or automation bias strip away from us our ideas of self-determinism. We may end up resigning to being a cog in the wheel, powerless to make choices.

In the aftermath of an adversity that has affected our performance, we may post-rationalise our fatalistic attitude in the following expressions:

'I knew it would happen!' Most commonly referred to as the 'I knew it all along' phenomenon, this captures our belief about our prior knowledge and ability to foresee now-factual incidents.

'It had to happen!' This hindsight bias refers to an attitude of resignation; fatalism makes us believe that incidents were inevitable.

'I said it would happen!' Post-incident, we tend to distort our recollection of earlier judgements retrospectively. An ambiguous, vague assumption of an

impending incident turns into a factual, explicit statement of truth. Hindsight bias post-incident distorts our readiness and preparedness to engage with future incidents. Egocentric reflections on past incidents, emphasising 'I', blind us to the warning signals that indicate another incident's imminence.

The toolbox

Escalation. Escalation processes enable us to deal with problems quickly and with clarity. Incorporated in incident management, escalations tend to define the involvement of more people to manage high-priority issues. The escalating process most often follows a hierarchical structure. That is to say, if we are unable to manage near-miss and actual incidents, these issues are escalated to more experienced or specialised people (see Figure 6.3).

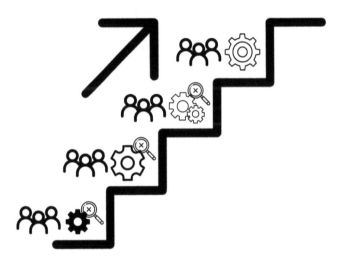

Figure 6.3 Escalation process.

An escalation process leans on the definition of decision categories that indicate different escalation pathways. For example, if we encounter a financial problem that we deem outside our control, these categories tell us which escalation procedure to activate, to whom to escalate, and what communications channels to experienced contributors and what specialised knowledge are needed in escalating.

The benefit of a well-specified, defined, and documented escalation process is that it minimises delays in making decisions. It drives accountability as well as focusing our attention on calling on the help of experienced and specialised people if we feel that we are unable to control an instance of significant difficulty on our own.

Blame

Once we have escalated a problem or issue, a speedy resolution may be hampered by the casting of blame. When something happens to go wrong, we tend to blame something or somebody else. Precious time is wasted addressing such questions as 'Who caused the problem?', 'Who could not deal with it in the first place?', or 'What went wrong?' We may 'pass the buck'; we ultimately hold others accountable, not us, and shift responsibility for dealing with the problem away from us.

Oversimplification

As much as we are inclined to oversimplify problems and solutions (see Chapter 4), we also tend to simplify the root cause, the foundation of the causal chain that resulted in the predicament we find ourselves in. The blame game may not only delay timely escalation but also focus attention on the illusion of a single initiating factor that triggered a chain. Ultimately, the process of escalation may only take us deep into a rabbit hole that confronts us with complexity that cannot be articulated straightforwardly. On the other hand, perhaps we oversimplify the circumstances of adversity to a level that provides us with a simplistic answer to why a problem needs to be escalated. Both these possibilities defeat the purpose of an escalation process – the quick resolution of a situation by a higher level of management or expertise.

Deference to authority

Hierarchical structures in an organisation often define an escalation channel; problems and issues are escalated to someone higher in rank and status (see Chapter 9). However, this higher authority may not necessarily have the expertise to provide an adequate resolution, nor may they be sensitive to the circumstances of the problem or issue and the consequences of their actions.

Escape

The primary purpose of escalating a problem or issue is to bring in additional authority and expertise. Nevertheless, the process may also be used to escalate responsibility and accountability away from us; let somebody else deal with the ramifications:

As much as people may generally prefer to maintain active control over their own decisions, they are also well-known to avoid choices when they become too difficult by deferring a decision or by choosing by default or omission (see Anderson, 2003, for a review), and even at times by delegating their choices to others.

(Steffel, Williams, and Perrmann-Graham, 2016, p. 32)

The negative facet of absolution is disempowerment. Additional authority and expertise may be parachuted in, stripping us of any remaining decision-making power. This forcible denial may result in considerable tensions.

 ## Centrifugal wisdom

Centripetal wisdom seems to dictate a stepwise abdication of ownership, responsibility, accountability, and thus control. It opens the door for us to pass the buck if we feel overwhelmed with the daunting task of anticipating and responding to near-miss and actual incidents.

In a high-reliability organisation, ownership of a problem and its resolution is paramount:

> … managers can mitigate risk … by requiring individuals to take responsibility for their actions and to indicate when they are unsure about decisions, situations, or other individuals or groups in the system. This concept ties in closely with the need for talk and communication. In distributed decision-making settings, articulating responsibility and ownership for outcomes helps mitigating risk because it creates a culture where "the buck stops everywhere". Thus, if an individual is uncertain, that fact must be communicated and the uncertainty addressed. Otherwise, uncertainty and risk increase, which can pull the system apart.

(Grabowski and Roberts, 1997, p. 157)

The 'buck that stops everywhere' is the antithesis of escalations; if we happen to be close to a problem, we own it until it is resolved.

Ownership

The determination of ownership is simple; we own the threat of a near-miss and actual incident adversely impacting aims, objectives, outcomes, and outputs important to the organisation. With an emphasis on the collective, we own the solution to it, regardless of whether we followed a process, procedure, or order or improvised our way out of the problem (see Chapter 5). Escalations as a way of allowing decision power to migrate away from the owner are discouraged.

Duty

Our job role may define what work activities we are responsible for. Let's widen such responsibility beyond our job role, so our duty and care are not bound by a narrow task orientation, but by a collective ownership of problems and issues. In essence, the definition of responsibility is widened beyond the mere obligation to do something, to be task-oriented along the lines of a job role. We commit ourselves to a duty to protect the collective from adversity, and thus to do what is professionally considered right.

Accountability

Hand in hand with the conventional interpretation of ownership and responsibility, we often hold individuals accountable to the extent to which they complete or do not complete a task or according to how obedient they are to a process, procedure, or routine. From a mindfulness perspective, accountability refers to the degree of answerability about whether a collective has done its best to anticipate and contain a near-miss or accident.

Engagement

The collective ownership of impending adversity requires the involvement and engagement of stakeholders (see Chapter 2) in the decision-making process. Anchoring everyone in the collective and taking everyone on a common journey of anticipating and responding to near-miss and actual incidents drives joint ownership and addresses the tensions that come from competing priorities.

Open communication

Maintaining collective ownership requires open real-time communication (see Chapter 8) that enables us to anticipate and respond to adversity early enough, before incidents snowball into a crisis or irrecoverable disaster. The wealth of information being transmitted may be presented as stories (see Chapter 2) to reinforce collective ownership and commitment towards action.

Noticing more

When we own a problem, we are more inclined to be more vigilant and more on the lookout. Owning a problem until it is resolved makes us stretch our minds (see Chapter 5), and makes us more discriminating (Chapter 4) in how we anticipate the unexpected:

> … when people enlarge their ability to act on problems, they also enlarge the range of issues they can now notice.

(Weick and Sutcliffe, 2015, p. 66)

Feedback and closure

Owning a problem until it is resolved will undoubtedly involve setbacks:

> If you experience infrequent setbacks then you have little experience opposing and ending such events. And if you are spared from the full force of collapse, failure, and disappointment, then you never learn the lesson that bad things come to an end. If you fail to learn the lessons of closure, then bad experiences, when they eventually do occur, can seem overwhelming. The feeling is one of "I can't handle this, it will never end, and I've got to escape from it.

(Weick and Sutcliffe, 2015, p. 118)

Hence, the continuing ownership of adversity requires a process of coming to terms with the fact that not all near-misses and accidents can be contained, let alone anticipated. An acceptance of materialising adversity enables us to move and continue to own the next challenge that lies ahead without ignoring the ramifications of a failure to maintain high-reliability performance.

The toolbox

Empowerment. In contrast to processes of escalation that can easily be abused as opportunities for absolution from responsibility and accountability, *"empowerment refers to a process whereby an individual's belief in his or her self-efficacy is enhanced"* (Conger and Kanungo, 1988, p. 474).

The process of empowerment suspends rigid hierarchical or rank and status-related structures (see Figure 6.4, and Chapter 9). Instead, it focuses in principle on enabling us to own the situation in a responsible and accountable manner.

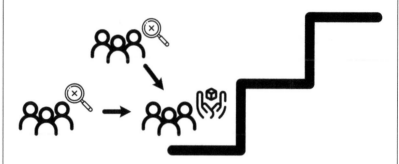

Figure 6.4 Empowerment process.

As a first step, we may explore the conditions that may result in us thinking that we are not in control of adversity anymore. Stretch zones (see Chapter 5) provide 'safe' spaces to hone skills and capabilities to think and critically engage with the (newly gained) freedom to act.

Once empowered, we need to rely on a wider range of information that must be relayed openly (see Chapter 4). The breadth and depth of our skills set, knowledge base, and range of accessible expertise need to be enhanced and enlarged to enable us to make the most informed judgements, genuinely owning the problem until it is resolved.

Culpability. As already mentioned, centripetal wisdom encourages inclinations for a quick exit so that we can dodge the bullet of accountability and blame. We may simply escalate a problem away from us so that others can pick up the pieces. Although the extent of escalations tells us how disempowered we were in the first place, centrifugal wisdom grants us a glimpse of the opposite, of empowerment that activates our stretch zone (see Chapter 5).

Nonetheless, the centrifugal wisdom of empowerment also demands a form of closure that allows us to own the problem until it is resolved and move on from near-misses and accidents that are, in principle, failures. As James Reason (1997, p. 207) argues:

> This 'hang them all' judgement is unsatisfactory in many respects. It ignores the ubiquity of error as well as the situational factors that promote it. Nor is it sensitive to the varieties of human failure and their different psychological origins.

Coming to terms with our influence to manage the fall-out from near-misses and accidents includes a judgement of culpability (see Figure 6.5).

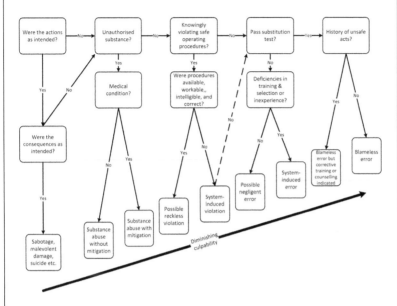

Figure 6.5 A decision tree for determining culpability for unsafe acts (Reason, 1997, p. 209).

In this figure, the 'substitution test' (Johnston, 1995) requires some explication:

> When faced with an accident or serious accident in which the unsafe acts of a particular person were implicated, we should perform the following mental test. Substitute the individual concerned for some-one else coming from the same domain of activity and possessing comparable qualifications and experience. Then ask the following question: 'In light of how events unfolded and were perceived by those involved in real time, is it likely that this new individual would have behaved any differently?'. If the answer is 'probably not' them as Johnston put it, '... apportioning blame has no material role to play, other than to obscure systemic deficiencies and to blame one of the victims'. A useful addition to the substitution test is to ask of the individual's peers: 'Given the circumstances that prevailed at the time, could you be sure that you would not have committed to the same or similar unsafe act? If the answer again is 'probably not', then blame is inappropriate.'

(Reason, 1997, p. 208)

Influencing - Revisiting the Airbus A380 development

In the late 1970s, the airline industry was marked by waves of deregulations. With fares and destinations open to competition, the dramatic rise of low-cost carriers reshaped an air travel market in a way that imposed considerable competitive pressure on legacy carriers.

The increasing demand for low-cost capacity drove Airbus to envisage the development of an ultra-high-capacity airliner to break the dominant market share of their flagship plane, the Boeing 747. Accordingly, in the late 1980s, Airbus commenced its development of the A380.

The multi-national nature of the development and manufacture of this behemoth soon ran it into trouble. At the heart of the problem was the reality that different design teams used different Computer-Aided Design software, resulting in partially incompatible and inconsistent design drawings. Faced with significant delays in 2005 and 2006, sheer complexity resulted in significant tensions between 16 design and production sites spread across France, Germany, Spain, and the United Kingdom. Escalations spiralled, costs mounted, and a political blame game, amplified by personal rivalries, compounded a perception of powerlessness and of progress being obstructed.

Eventually, the problem of interoperability was solved, and on 15 October 2007, the first A380–800 was delivered to Singapore Airlines. The media hailed A380 as a marvel of engineering and yet were already sceptical about its success:

> The A380 is a massive airplane with a length not much more than a 747-400, but a girth that looks like someone jammed a dozen elephants under the skin.

> What amazed me was the comprehensive technological demonstration the aircraft put on as it passed overhead.

> Surely the airplane was not at a maximum weight, but even with all the drag it surely commanded a fair amount of power to cross the threshold. And from the noise perspective passing over head, as well as the noise it generated when it went into reverse after landing, the A380, will be a very quiet, yet formidable competitor.

> There's certainly plenty that has gone right in the process that brought the A380 to Chicago this week, but thousands of detours have slowed the process as well, much as it might have with anyone who assumes the risks of building airplanes today. One problem is a massive credibility gap at Airbus between what the company promises and with it can deliver.

(Simons, 2014, p. 160)

Once in service in 2007, two years later than planned, the A380 was beset with some teething issues. Although these were ironed out over time, the aircraft's poor economics signalled the beginning of its end. Its running costs have been roughly equal to that of two 787s. Subsequently, airlines gradually opted for smaller, more fuel-efficient planes that provided them with greater flexibility. The demand for the A380 dried up, and on 14 February 2019, Airbus announced the end of the A380.

Just-this-way and just-for-now

Our biases may tempt us to believe that we are increasingly powerless in the face of ongoing near-misses and actual incidents. The temptation may overtake us, enticing us to delegate or escalate responsibility and accountability away from us, attributing our lack of ownership to other people or events that are perceived to be outside our control. According to conventional wisdom, when we start acknowledging our limitations, we can trigger the process of delegation and escalation.

So, the mind-boggling complexity of the A380 development became increasingly paralysing. The just-this-way (see Figure 6.6) style of working was one of attributing blame and finger-pointing, and progressively the prospect of a 'great escape' through escalations became the norm.

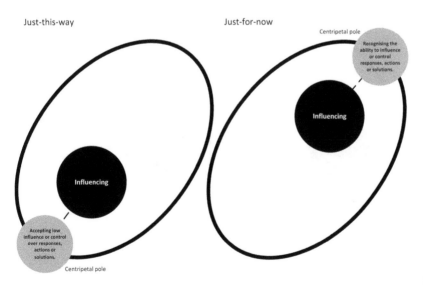

Figure 6.6 Just-this-way and just-for-now polarity (influencing).

That is not to say that, just-for-now, there weren't occasional designers and managers who stepped into the breach and tried to own a worsening trajectory in the development of the A380. Nevertheless, their recognition of their own ability to influence and control the materialising adversity was severely hampered by the limited extent of their authority.

Both the extremes of the poles displayed in Figure 6.6 are to be avoided. Either our management of near-misses and accidents results in a 'merry-go-round' of time-intensive escalations, or we cling on to an illusory belief that only we can own and resolve impending adversity, until it is too late.

Just-in-case and just-in-time

A third both/and, just-in-case course of action is one of integration. To respond to near-misses and actual incidents in an early, timely manner, we need to widen and deepen the sphere of our ability to influence the management of looming adversity. We own the problem until it is ironed out. However, even when we have identified and appreciated the limits of our control and influence, we are still left with an opportunity to escalate.

Integrating both poles into a third way (see Figure 6.7) is valuable as, first, appreciation of our limitations in influencing and controlling impending adversity in the form of near-misses and accidents leads to timely deference (see Chapter 9) to additional expertise, or an investment in widening our response repertoire in

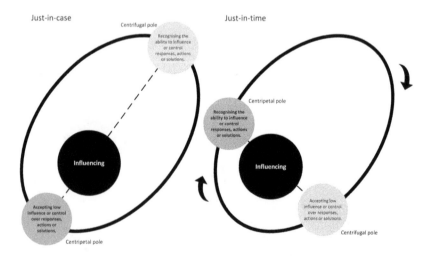

Figure 6.7 Just-in-case and just-in-time polarity (influencing).

the long term. Second, taking the centrifugal pole into account, through building up expertise, skills, and capabilities to deal with adversity, we may be able to see that there is no need for escalations from the outset.

The integration of both poles provides a nuanced approach to offset the lure of abdicating responsibility as well as the urge to cling to managing adversity in a situation perceived as hopeless:

JUST-IN-CASE, we intend to own a problem WHILE honouring our limitations of influence and control. Owning adversity does not imply that we have to showcase our assertiveness and decisiveness as a lone ranger: a person supposed to have superior intellect and skills who stands alone but is always expected to come out on top in every situation. An empowered collective, a team, for example, is one in which we care for each other, which is committed to a shared goal-setting and driven by an appropriate reward system that balances individual and collective accomplishments as well as sharing the ramifications of collective failures. We are aware of our limitations and we are not reluctant to ask for help.

JUST-IN-CASE, we assume authority WHILE recognising the boundaries of actions. Empowering collectives for driving ownership may well be interpreted as free-for-all decision-making. Although spontaneity and improvisational practices are encouraged, boundaries need to be set, preferably within the realms of a stretch zone (see Chapter 5).

Also, empowering a collective does not imply a disregard for individual responsibilities and accountabilities. On the contrary, although individual responsibility and accountability boundaries may become blurred in the intricacies of collective organising, they still need to be clearly defined, and interdependencies between people highlighted and scrutinised.

JUST-IN-CASE, we defer to authority, rank, and status WHILE assuming power to deviate from rules, routines, procedures, and policies. Due to our inherent bias towards overestimating our ability to control and underestimating the extent to which adversity is threatening the course of action we have taken, we tend not to trigger a process of escalation early enough. Instead, we keep intact the illusory belief that no one but us can anticipate and respond to near-misses and actual incidents; until it is too late.

These just-in-case principles might match your idea of combining two opposing poles that yield benefits in managing adversity. The challenge is in the notion of setting these principles in stone. Let us attempt to bolt on a condition that defines the extent to which we adhere to it:

JUST-IN-CASE, we intend to own a problem WHILE honouring our limitations of influence and control, AS LONG AS we are appreciative that escalations to rank and status do not provide a hastened closure. Although escalations are discouraged, we may find ourselves in a situation where clinging to the problem turns into a futile exercise. The conditions under which one may escalate, in the conventional fashion, up hierarchical structures to activate additional resources, skills, and capabilities, and fresh perspectives (see Chapters 9 and 10) need to be defined. In extremity, this may involve the replacement of the owners of a problem or issue.

Towards a paradox mindset

A typical response to us losing control might trigger a process of escalation. If we do not keep a lid on processes and escalations, we could also trigger a game of deflecting blame. That would begin with the search for an elusive root cause that remains essentially fictitious in the wicked contexts in which we tend to operate.

To align ourselves with the opposite pole of the dualism of escalation, we can trigger a process of empowerment to infuse a collective with initiative. In itself, the mere principle of empowerment may drive out-of-control decision-making, while at the same time contributing to it, if it is allowed to unravel unchecked, with no imposed boundaries.

So, ultimately, the right approach may reside, just-in-time, somewhere in between the two polar opposites of escalating and owning.

References

Conger, J. A. and Kanungo, R. N. (1988) 'The empowerment process: Integrating theory and practice', *Academy of Management Review*, 13(3), pp. 471–482.

Grabowski, M. and Roberts, K. (1997) 'Risk mitigation in large-scale systems: Lessons from high reliability organisations', *California Management Review*, 39(4), pp. 152–161.

Johnston, N. (1995) 'Do blame and punishment have a role in organisational risk management?', *Flight Deck*, 15, pp. 33–36.

Liu, X. and Sun, L. (2021) 'Examining the impact of fatalism belief and optimism orientation on seismic preparedness: Considering their roles in the nexus between risk perception and preparedness', *Journal of Contingencies and Crisis Management*, In Press.

Masys, A. (2015) 'Preface', in Masys, A. (ed.) *Disaster management: Enabling resilience*. London: Springer, pp. v–xiii.

Reason, J. (1997) *Managing the risks of organisational accidents*. Aldershot: Ashgate.

Saha, J. M. (2006) *Management and organisational behaviour*. Chicago, IL: Excel Books.

Simons, G. (2014) *The Airbus A380: A history*. Barnsley: Pen & Sword Aviation.

Steffel, M., Williams, E. F. and Perrmann-Graham, J. (2016) 'Passing the buck: Delegating choices to others to avoid responsibility and blame', *Organizational Behavior and Human Decision Processes*, 135, pp. 32–44.

Weick, K. and Sutcliffe, K. (2015) *Managing the unexpected: Sustained performance in a complex world*. 3rd edn. Hoboken, NJ: Wiley.

Chapter 7

Aligning responses

A variety of biases, inclinations, and preferences make us believe that we as individuals are infallible in our ability to deal with adversity single-handedly. We take decisions unilaterally, ignoring the need for shared and coordinated decisions. The threshold of unilateral action is further deepened by the necessity to work in a group.

Misaligned, fragmented responses from multiple individuals result in tensions that may jeopardise successful coordination and collaboration towards a common goal. A response from one individual may counter one from somebody else, and thus collective sensemaking is at stake:

> This occurs when, for example, two people interact and make sense of the nonobvious in ways that neither of them alone could have done. Their sense, as well as their organising, are emergent adaptations that are more tailored to the present context and less constrained by whatever the individuals separately bring to the situation.

(Weick and Sutcliffe, 2015, p. 68)

The major challenge is to drive coherence as a reasonable and logical fit between responses that are directed at anticipating and responding to near-misses and accidents (see Figure 7.1).

Figure 7.1 Complexity in decision-making.

DOI: 10.4324/9781003083115-7

Such coherence indicates how to integrate complex interactions between differ-ent individuals and the mental and physical aspects of the task. Responding to impending adversity may pose a dilemma. Shall we unilaterally respond to the incident so no time is wasted, or instead align our actions in a collaborative and coordinated manner (see Figure 7.2)?

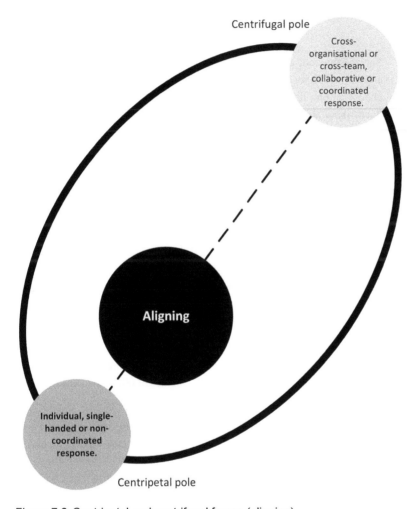

Centrifugal pole

Cross-organisational or cross-team, collaborative or coordinated response.

Aligning

Individual, single-handed or non-coordinated response.

Centripetal pole

Figure 7.2 Centripetal and centrifugal forces (aligning).

Centripetal wisdom

Our egocentric tendencies make us believe that we alone deploy the only 'right' response to a near-miss or accident. It becomes self-evidently correct that our

123

stand-alone work is in line with a plan, falls into place, and forges plausible coherence in an environment defined by response complexity.

A variety of biases, inclinations, and preferences make us believe that we as individuals are infallible in our ability to deal with adversity single-handedly. We take decisions unilaterally, ignoring the need for shared and coordinated decisions. The threshold of unilateral action is further deepened by the necessity to work in a group:

> Social behaviour does not represent a simple aggregation of personal preferences or dispositions; our choices are often interdependent. When we choose among lines of action, our decisions often are predicated on inferences about others' preferences and intentions.

> (Kitts, 2003, p. 222)

False consensus. The false consensus effect (Ross, Greene, and House, 1977) makes us believe that others commonly share our qualities, characteristics, beliefs, and actions. Thus, we assume greater validity and support for our own position. If a general agreement is questioned, we thus lean towards discounting such challenging views.

Illusion of asymmetric insight. In short, the illusion of asymmetric insight (Pronin *et al.*, 2001) explains why we leave our responses relatively unchecked and under-scrutinised, as we believe we know better than others.

Uniqueness bias. Those who believe themselves to be exhibiting desirable behaviour gravitate towards underestimating the extent to which others are doing the same. In contrast, if we believe that our response is undesirable, objectionable, or unsatisfactory, we overestimate the number of others also engaged with 'bad' behaviour (Suls, Wan, and Sanders, 1988).

Illusion. We tend to overestimate our ability to exercise influence on events (Anderson, 1976). We may even claim responsibility (see Hindsight bias in Chapter 2) for past incidents to which no causal link can be demonstrated. As a consequence, we can claim a greater internal locus of control (see Chapter 6) than we actually have.

The degree to which we create an illusion of control is partly influenced by self-efficacy (Bandura, 1977) – our own personal judgment of how well we can cope with a situation in light of our skills and the circumstances we face:

Efficacy expectations vary on several dimensions that have important performance implications. They differ in magnitude. Thus when tasks are ordered in level of difficulty, the efficacy expectations of different individuals may be limited to the simpler tasks, extend to moderately difficult ones, or include the most taxing performances. Efficacy expectations also differ in generality. Some experiences create circumscribed mastery expectations. Others instill more a generalised sense of efficacy that extends well beyond the specific treatment situation. In addition, expectancies vary in strength. Weak expectations are easily extinguishable by disconfirming experiences, whereas individuals who process strong expectations of mastery will persevere in their coping efforts despite disconfirming experiences.

(Bandura, 1977, p. 194)

Superiority. The illusory effect of self-efficacy tends to be amplified by our longing to feel superior to other people. Illusory superiority (Hoorens, 1993) draws on our competitive nature and may result in us overestimating our desirable qualities and abilities compared with those of other people.

All aforementioned biases, inclinations, and preferences mark an unmistakable belief that we know better. The question of why we do something is being suppressed; what we are doing becomes paramount. Our top priority is to 'zoom-in' (see Figure 7.3), to be task-oriented and as productive as possible in managing near-misses and accidents.

Figure 7.3 Zooming-in.

In other words, we call the shots based on our supposedly superior knowledge and expertise and act on the assumption in a 'closing-in' manner:

> Close-in managers look for immediate benefits and make ad hoc decisions. They often favour one-on-one conversations over group meetings. They want to address details by doing whatever occurs to them. Faced with a problem, they look for quick fixes rather than stand back to seek underlying causes, alternatives, or long-term solutions. They prefer to contact someone they know rather than search more widely for expertise. These tendencies are exacerbated in organisations that restrict information flow, reward quick hits, and confine people to their roles.

(Kanter, 2011, p. 3)

The toolbox

To-do lists. To-do lists facilitate zooming-in on having full command of what tasks are necessary in order to anticipate and contain impending adversity. Plans, schedules, and deadlines are broken down into tasks we adhere to in a compliant fashion (see Chapter 5). In a mainly reductionist manner (see Figure 7.4), we zoom-in to the task at hand and focus our attention on mastering that task (see Chapter 6).

Figure 7.4 Aligning as a checklist approach.

To-do lists are generally accompanied by productivity timers, time planners, and rigid deadlines that determine the completion of a task. They tend to set out urgent, prioritised tasks in the most precise manner. Nevertheless, such lists should not be mistaken for the checklist mentioned in Chapter 5.

Although similarly reductionist, a checklist is about ticking off procedures that we carry out daily in a routine manner. On the other hand, a to-do list is more customised to certain tasks that need to be addressed while exercising and 'ticking off' those procedures promoted by the checklist.

Being task-oriented and focused through trusting to-do lists and timers is beneficial in concentrating our attention on being consistently productive (where our actions and responses are determined by checklists). Moreover, this helps to set expectations as it defines clear parameters of in/activity and task in/completion.

Silo mentality

Zooming-in increases silo thinking. Information about the task is 'siloed' and stockpiled for carrying out the task efficiently. This may allow us independent working, but it constrains the free flow of information (see Chapter 8) and thus limits the extent to which we and others are sensitive to the implications of our actions:

> The significance of this feature [Sensitivity] can be seen by contrasting it with the situation in many organisations where 'silo' thinking prevails, that is, where employees operate within their own small sphere of influence without thought of the more remote impact of their activities. A culture of silos has been implicated in many organisational accidents.

> (Hopkins, 2009, p. 13)

Competition

Egocentric tendencies to want to master a task reinforce our own perceptions and opinions on how to carry out a task better and more rapidly and cost-effectively than others. Fortifying a silo mentality, unadulterated task orientation weakens our willingness to recognise the needs of others as we see each other as competitors. In extreme circumstances, beyond acting out of the desire for recognition, admiration, and adulation, tasks may be completed for more sinister purposes, to manipulate others.

Lowering the bar

Because we are inclined to know better than others, not only because of our egocentric tendencies but also because we are valued according to how productive we are, we may lower the bar of plausibility so that, for example, we can move on to the next task. Why question or re-evaluate the task or its implementation if it has been imposed on us as at the request of a higher authority? As long as we can 'tick the box' to suggest we have carried out the task, we can proceed to the next.

It is not surprising that, because of these tendencies, we gravitate towards lowering the bar of plausibility we attach to any response we require in order to move on. In the case of the Bhopal disaster, considered one of the world's worst industrial disasters, Weick (2010, p. 549) commented:

> When they deal with ambiguity, interdependent people search for meaning, settle for plausibility, and move on. The operating crew at Bhopal search for the meaning of the smell of boiled cabbage, plausibly label it as the odour of mosquito spray, and move on to drink tea. This represents sensemaking with a low bar for plausibility put in place by crude concepts, coarse-grained perception, and experience within a deteriorating plant.

Subordination

Ticking off a to-do or checklist may be all we need to do or all we have to ask others to do. Still, this opens the door for us to disintegrate into zooming-in, task-oriented individuals who seek to maintain the status quo by simply ticking off these lists through subordination:

> Subordination refers to the condition in which people treat the system as their dominant context, ask what it needs, and act in ways intended to meet those needs. Less heedful subordination occurs when people work to rule, partition the world into my job and not my job, largely based on self-interest, and spend more time talking than listening.

(Weick and Sutcliffe, 2015, p. 85)

Commitment

We may expend considerable effort on mastering a task that we believe makes no difference at all in the end if we have lost sight of a bigger picture – or never established one in the first place. It may not matter to us and others if we have completed the task or not. Correspondingly, our commitment to do well in carrying out a task may be lessened (see Chapter 6) so that we can focus on tasks that are more enjoyable.

Centrifugal wisdom

Centripetal wisdom expresses a propensity to zoom-in on clear or obvious tasks without needing any proof, explanation, or harmonious adjustment and alignment with other people or groups. Whereas isolated task orientation makes us look at responses up close, aligning those requirements means having to zoom-out to see responses to emerging adversity from afar; people act and diagnose problems and respond to these problems iteratively (Weick and Sutcliffe, 2015).

The practice of heedful interrelating best epitomises the process of aligning in high-reliability organisations:

> Heedful interrelating is a social process through which individual action contributes to a larger pattern of shared action. The pattern of shared action is a threefold combination of contributions, representations, and subordination (Weick 2009, 164). That is, when people interrelate heedfully, they first understand how a system is configured to achieve some goal, and they see their work as a contribution to the system and not as a standalone activity. Second, they see how their job fits with other people's jobs to accomplish the goals of the system (they visualise the meshing of mutually dependent contributions). And third, they maintain a conscious awareness of both as they perform their duties. Although a simplification, one way to better understand heedful interrelating is by considering its opposite, heedless interrelating – when people simply do their jobs without considering how their work contributes to the overall outcome and ignoring what is going on around them, both upstream and downstream.

> (Sutcliffe, 2018, p. 70)

In other words, we act and diagnose iteratively when anticipating and responding to near-miss and actual incidents. We align our actions to those of others while creating an awareness of how all these actions fit together and how the ramifications can spread to other areas. In high-reliability organisations, we simultaneously zoom-in and zoom-out (see Figure 7.5).

Figure 7.5 Zooming-in, zooming-out.

Multiple perspectives

To address any stakeholder ambiguity (see Chapter 2), the activity of zooming-out should not just include one own's perspective but also those of other stake-holders. This, of course, poses a challenge if stakeholders cannot specify and clarify their own perspectives. As a consequence, stakeholder ambiguity may well increase through zooming-out activities. Therefore, embrace it by engaging with other stakeholders' perspectives, rather than oversimplifying it by relying solely on your own (see Chapter 4).

Increasing scrutiny

Zooming-out may not matter in the first instance because we, with our egocentric tendencies, believe that any response we make is self-evidently correct. Thus, we lower the bar of plausibility to move on to zooming into the next task. So, our sensitivity to the wider environment and individual tasks should be guided by actionable questions (Weick and Sutcliffe, 2015), such as those in Table 7.1. Keep asking yourself questions such as 'Why?', 'So What?', 'What for?', or 'Now what?'.

Frontline zooming-in and zooming-out

Commonly, those people at the operational frontline are charged with being task-oriented:

> Make sure to reward managers who stay close to the operating system or frontline activities. Managers who demonstrate ongoing attention to operations create a context where surprises are more likely to be spotted and corrected before they grow into problems.

(Weick and Sutcliffe, 2015, p. 93)

Being sensitive doesn't simply mean being in a solely zoomed-in mindset. It also means being encouraged, incentivised, and rewarded to combine task-oriented practices with, for example, big-picture thinking (see the Textbox below).

Moving targets

Traditional probabilistic risk management (see Chapters 3 and 4) promotes a past-informed, task-oriented to-do list. The activity is usually carried out just once, establishing a holistic but static view of risks; then this to-do list of managing risks is applied and worked through in a prioritised manner, informed by probabilities and impact. If we zoom-in, it remains essential to update our understanding of the dynamic nature of risks and how we respond to them; we need to update the bigger picture by real-time zooming-out. This requires constant communication (see Chapter 8) that is not slowed down by bureaucratic hurdles.

Ownership

It is not difficult to dismiss the alignment of our actions to others as inconsequential and thus irrelevant, as we can escalate the consequences of our actions or inaction to somebody else (see Chapter 6). However, when we zoom-out, we own the resulting big picture (see the following textbox) in all its complexity and ambiguity.

The toolbox

Big pictures. Zooming-out from a narrow task-focus is often associated with the framing of a big picture. Those of us who are inclined to adhere to big-picture thinking are said to be creative, but also disorganised. The other extreme relates to those who are preoccupied with task orientation. These people tend to be labelled as planners, as diligent, and meticulous, but they may lack the wider perspective, the helicopter view.

The previous chapter offered a range of big pictures as diverse as a risk register or a set of scenarios. A big picture may not be a tangible representation of a wider perspective, but rather a mental image or impression one has:

> Those who man the combat operations centers of US Navy Ships use the term 'having the bubble' to indicate that they have been able to construct and maintain the cognitive map that allows them to integrate such diverse inputs as combat status, information sensors, remote observation, and the real-time status and performance of the various weapons and systems into a single picture of the ship's overall situation and operational status.

(Rochlin, 1997, p. 109)

131

Whatever your big picture is, it enables us to zoom-out beyond the mere task, allowing us to holistically assess a situation and align our individual contributions with others (see Figure 7.6).

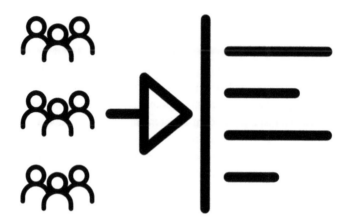

Figure 7.6 Alignment of us to others.

By engaging with big-picture thinking, we may address a plethora of questions, such as:

• If I did this, what would be the unintended consequences?

• Is there anybody who might be affected by my actions?

• What would the failure to carry out a task mean in the bigger picture?

Big-picture thinking can be done individually, but it is more beneficial to engage with collective big-picture thinking. Not only does it reveal differences in angles and perspectives but it also raises the important question of what it is that I am not asking myself.

Aligning - Revisiting the Volkswagen emission scandal

In September 2015, Volkswagen AG, by then the biggest car manufacturer in the world, got embroiled in an emission scandal. Up to 11 million cars worldwide had been equipped with an illegal software, a 'defeat device' that falsely recorded lower nitrogen oxide (NOx) emissions in order to satisfy testing agencies in the United States and Europe. The hidden damage from these VW vehicles could equate to all of the United Kingdom's yearly NOx emissions from all power stations, vehicles, industry, and agriculture. The organisational damage was equally astounding. The overall bill to Volkswagen to cover fixes to the affected cars, penalties, and potential customer compensation could amount to $25 billion.

In 1993, Ferdinand Piëch became the chairman of Volkswagen. At that time, Volkswagen was close to bankruptcy, and Piëch was central to the turnaround. In the following years, he up-marketed the Volkswagen and Audi brands with great success. By acquiring such brands as Lamborghini, Rolls-Royce, and Bentley, he turned Volkswagen into a global player.

Despite these successes, Piëch was also known for his autocratic style of leadership and his need to micro-manage the operations of Volkswagen. His centralised way of decision-making, informed by a group of advisors, created a 'climate of fear'. Those who did not meet his aggressive sales targets would have to leave the organisation. The supervisory function in the organisation, primarily through the supervisory board but also through investors and shareholders, had no significant independent voice. In short, what Piëch said was not to be questioned or simply could not be questioned.

Just-this-way and just-for-now

By default, we are prone to engage with impending adversity heroically, driven by a notion of superiority or simply by the ticking of the clock while knowing that something has to be done quickly. The urge to single-handedly decide may be intensified by authority, rank, and status.

Therefore, it may not be so startling that Volkswagen was essentially a 'one-man-show' anchored by a single 'cannot fail' big picture. Just-this-way, the CEO called the shots and subordinated his workforce to do what he thought was right, no matter what the consequences were. Volkswagen became the world's best-selling automaker by being bold, assertive, and uniquely independent. The just-this-way (see Figure 7.7) mentality paid off, no matter what it took. This mantra was hammered home through the hierarchy. The shots were called at the top of Volkswagen in the erroneous belief that the external environment would not be aware of that, would not dissent, and would ultimately fall in line with whatever Volkswagen did.

The opposite just-for-now pole, one of collaboration and coordination with external regulators such as the US Environmental Protection Agency, only took hold once the emission scandal was made public, although the damage was already done. Nevertheless, although the Volkswagen brand was damaged and the diesel emission scandal cost the company in excess of $30 billion, in 2021, the CEO of the Volkswagen group commented:

We're keeping up our high pace, both operationally and strategically. The record result in the first half of the year is clear proof of how strong our brands are and how attractive their products are. The premium segment performed especially well with double-digit returns, as did Financial Services. Our electric offensive is picking up momentum and we will keep on increasing its pace in the months to come. We are also realigning the company with our new Group strategy NEW AUTO so that we can tap future profit pools. In doing so, we are preparing Volkswagen to play a leading role in the new world of mobility.

(Volkswagen Group News, 2021)

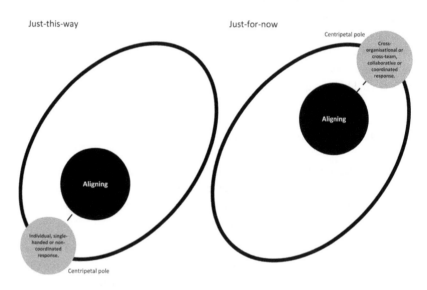

Figure 7.7 Just-this-way and just-for-now polarity (aligning).

Just-in-case and just-in-time

It seems sensible to embrace both poles, moving on from extremes of just-this-way and just-for-now. On one hand, blocking out what is happening around us and taking unilateral actions on the back of our superior belief allows us to make quick decisions. On the other, in contrast, the processes and practices of coordination and collaboration enable us to align our actions with those of other internal and external organisational entities, reducing tensions and conflict. Ergo, just-in-case (see Figure 7.8), let's embrace both poles.

Let's assume that one of us has to decide and act in the end and – with a view to meeting deadlines, being first to market, or preventing a near-miss and accident from cascading into a crisis – act quickly and decisively, while always being sensitive to the ramifications of our actions.

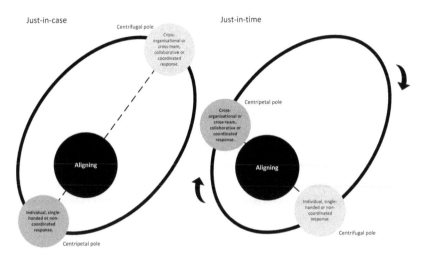

Figure 7.8 Just-this-way and just-for-now polarity (aligning).

To describe this balance in more detail, the following principles may be useful:

JUST-IN-CASE, we wish to decide unilaterally WHILE being sensitive to the consequences of our actions. We hold dear the principles of being decisive and acting quickly, taking into account the warning signals of impending adversity (see Chapter 3), while always having a bigger picture in mind that tells us what matters most. Constant zooming-in and zooming-out from this bigger picture allows us to put action into perspective.

JUST-IN-CASE, we aspire to delegate a task WHILE making sure to convey the big picture(s). Considering that we may not have the capacity or capability to carry out all tasks necessary to manage near-misses and accidents, we may delegate or escalate (see Chapter 6) those tasks to other people with greater experience (see Chapter 9). We should not forget to pass on the bigger picture(s) to the task recipient in order to make sure the task is not carried out mindlessly, devoid of any recognition of the need for coordination and collaboration.

JUST-IN-CASE, we crave to be task-oriented WHILE creating space to zoom-out. We tend to be assessed by the extent to which we are productive; by the degree to which we complete tasks efficiently. Granting that actions need to be taken and tasks to be completed, we need to create some space for us and others to zoom-out, so we can align with each other.

To add a dynamic dimension to such principles, just-in-time, the first of these might be further expanded as follows:

JUST-IN-TIME, we wish to decide unilaterally WHILE being sensitive to the consequences of our actions, AS LONG AS we are within the boundaries of our response repository. With reference to Chapter 6, we can empower ourselves to do anything we like as we believe we know the ramifications of our actions. However, we may not be the experts who can do all we think is needed most competently. Accordingly, the first just-in-case principle needs to be further bounded by the extent to which we are empowered to think and act (see Chapter 5).

Towards a paradox mindset

Ending with a complex just-in-time principle may result in cognitive overload, confusion, and perplexity. Please define your principles so that they are not overly simplified but also so that they are not difficult to understand, to clarify and thus to apply. So that you don't become 'stuck' (Kanter, 2011) in a zoomed-in or zoomed-out perspective, the following table (Table 7.1) raises a range of probing questions:

Table 7.1 Zooming-In, Zooming-Out (adapted by Kanter, 2011)

Are You Stuck in a Perspective That's Too Far in?		Are You Stuck in a Perspective That's Too Far out?	
Telltale Signs	Questions That Will Help You Zoom-out	Telltale Signs	Questions That Will Help You Zoom-in
You get overwhelmed by countless details	What is the context? What matters most?	You dismiss deviations from plans or models as too minor to matter	Does the deviation challenge the model? How can the deviation be understood?
You take things personally, finding the 'me' angle first	What larger purpose is being served? What is at stake for others?	You veer away from dealing with specific problems in favour of focusing on general theory	What actions does your theory suggest for a particular problem?
You trade favours, hoping others will 'do it for me'	Why is the task or mission worthy of support?	You must have a full analysis or a big study before determining actions	Is there sufficient information to proceed in this instance? What are the costs of delay?

(Continued)

Are You Stuck in a Perspective That's Too Far in?		Are You Stuck in a Perspective That's Too Far out?	
Telltale Signs	Questions That Will Help You Zoom-out	Telltale Signs	Questions That Will Help You Zoom-in
You make exceptions or special deals based on particular circumstances	Will the circumstances recur? What policies or decision frameworks could be used?	You always stay on major established paths	Are there side roads or shortcuts?
You jump on any good-looking offer that pops up	Does this fit the goal or destination? What else might be on the horizon?	You pursue the mission regardless of the human costs	How is this affecting the people who must carry out the mission?
You treat every situation as unique	Are there other similar situations? What categories or groupings make sense?	You fit everything into a few general categories	What are the details that make things different? Which details matter?

What working principles can you define that combine and integrate the need to respond to impending adversity unilaterally and single-handedly while being more sensitive to the consequences of your decisions and actions?

References

Anderson, C. R. (1976) 'Locus of control, coping behaviors, and performance in a stress setting: A longitudinal study', *Journal of Applied Psychology*, 62(4), pp. 446–451.

Bandura, A. (1977) 'Self-efficacy: Toward a unifying theory of behavioral change', *Psychological Review*, 84(2), pp. 191–215.

Hoorens, V. (1993) 'Self-enhancement and superiority biases in social comparison', *European Review of Social Psychology*, 4(1), pp. 113–139.

Hopkins, A. (2009) 'Identifying and responding to warnings', in Hopkins, A. (ed.) *Learning from high reliability organisations*. North Ryde: CCH Australia, pp. 33–58.

Kanter, R. M. (2011) 'Managing yourself: Zoom in, zoom out', *Harvard Business Review*, 89(3), pp. 112–116.

Kitts, J. A. (2003) 'Egocentric bias or information management? Selective disclosure and the social roots of norm misperception', *Social Psychology Quarterly*, 66(3), pp. 222–237.

Pronin, E. *et al.* (2001) 'You don't know me, but I know you: The illusion of asymmetric insight', *Journal of Personality and Social Psychology*, 81(4), pp. 639–656.

Rochlin, G. I. (1997) *Trapped in the net: The unanticipated consequences of computerization.* Princeton, NJ: Princeton University Press.

Ross, L., Greene, D. and House, P. (1977) 'The "false consensus effect": An egocentric bias in social perception and attribution processes', *Journal of Experimental Social Psychology*, 13(3), pp. 279–301.

Suls, J., Wan, C. K. and Sanders, G. S. (1988) 'False consensus and false uniqueness in estimating the prevalence of health-protective behaviors', *Journal of Applied Social Psychology*, 18(1), pp. 66–79.

Sutcliffe, K. (2018) 'Mindful organizing', in Ramanujam, R. and Roberts, K. H. (eds.) *Organizing for reliability: A guide for research and practice.* Stanford, CA: Stanford University Press, pp. 61–89.

Volkswagen Group News (2021) *Volkswagen Group raises outlook for 2021 after a record result in the first half of the year.* Available at: https://www.volkswagen-newsroom.com/en/press-releases/volkswagen-group-raises-outlook-for-2021-after-a-record-result-in-the-first-half-of-the-year-7375.

Weick, K. (2010) 'Reflections on enacted sensemaking in the Bhopal disaster', *Journal of Management Studies*, 47(3), 537–550.

Weick, K. and Sutcliffe, K. (2015) *Managing the unexpected: Sustained performance in a complex world.* 3rd edn. Hoboken, NJ: Wiley.

Weick, K. E. (2009) *Making sense of the organization: The impermanent organization.* Chichester: Wiley.

Chapter 8

Communicating with others

In its simplest form, communication is an ongoing process of coding and decoding of verbal (e.g. speech, writings such as letters, emails, notes, texts, and billboards) and non-verbal (e.g. tone of voice, body language, symbols, and pictorial) messages. In addition, there are two principal communication types that could be classified as formal and informal communication. Formal communication is confined to the 'official' channels that cross-organisational structures vertically, horizontally, or diagonally. In contrast, informal communication is characterised by casual ad-hoc interactions.

Figure 8.1 Coding and decoding in communication.

The major challenge of communication is that the meaning and significance of a message (see Figure 8.1) may get lost. With the process of coding and decoding, biases creep in and distort the message that we want to convey:

> We all have a natural urge to judge, evaluate, and approve (or disapprove) another person's statement. Suppose someone, commenting on what I have just stated says, "I did not like what that man said." How will you respond? Almost invariably, your reply will be either approval or disapproval of the attitude expressed. Either you respond, "I didn't either; I thought it was terrible," or else you say, "Oh, I thought it was really good." In other words, your first reaction is to evaluate it from your point of view.
>
> (Rogers and Roethlisberger, 1952, p. 105)

Hence, the (de)coding process reveals sender and receiver biases that are problematic in the creation of a shared understanding of how to anticipate and respond to impending incidents.

DOI: 10.4324/9781003083115-8

Figure 8.2 shows the bipolar opposites that we as managers face when it comes to communicating about impending adversity. On one hand, we are tempted to limit and restrict our communication. On the other, in stark opposition to the centripetal pole, we may want to share information extensively, transparently, and openly.

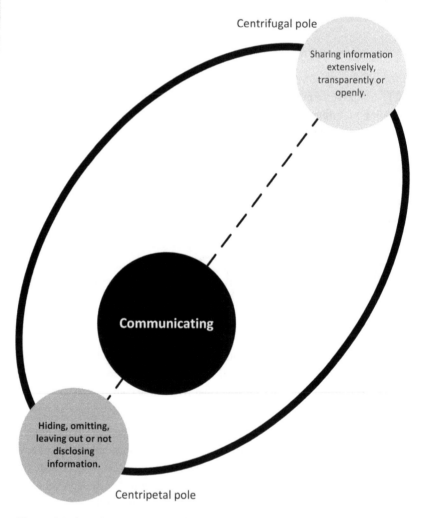

Centrifugal pole

Sharing information extensively, transparently or openly.

Communicating

Hiding, omitting, leaving out or not disclosing information.

Centripetal pole

Figure 8.2 Centripetal and centrifugal forces (communicating).

 **Centripetal wisdom**

Our ability to communicate with each other has changed drastically over recent years. Facilitated by technology, we can transmit and receive an infinite volume of information. Instead of being constrained to talk to a limited number of people in person, we can now communicate to anyone, anywhere in the world, anytime. A paradoxical tendency is that although we have technological means at hand to communicate an ever greater amount of information, we are inclined to share less, replacing informal verbal and non-verbal communication with abbreviated written messaging. We are increasingly tempted to curb the extent to which we communicate with each other; by sending a text or posting a message on social media instead of having an actual, physical conversation.

It is not surprising that the following dispositions further cloud our communication of impending adversity:

To whom it is communicated. People want to believe others they are familiar with, who they trust, despite any evidence to the contrary. Truth bias (Levine, 2014) is associated with belief in the sender of a message. By default, we are inclined to presume that other people are honest in their communication. The possibility of dishonesty or deception is suppressed.

How we communicate a message. The framing effect (Druckman, 2001) says that because of 'how' a message is conveyed, we may tend to undervalue 'what' has been said. Hence, we may choose an option that is worse than any that was actually contained in the message.

How often a message is repeated. The more often we hear the same message, the greater is our tendency to believe it. Repeated exposure to a message results in a perception of greater familiarity and to positive connotations associated with the message. The illusory truth effect (Fazio *et al.*, 2015) is further amplified if the message aligns with our preconceived ideas of what we want to believe.

Centripetal wisdom suggests a trend toward the abbreviation and abstraction of communication in a formalised setting to create snippets of non-verbal messages that are concise, compelling, simple, and memorable, and that largely avoid the biases or predispositions mentioned above. Such an approach is more efficient, as it allows us to increase the transmission and retention of messages.

Keep it short, simple, and consistent

'Keep it simple stupid!' is only one mantra that defines modern communication. Keeping consistent messaging short and simple enables us to transmit more messages in a more assertive manner. The drawback of such an approach is that we create snippets of information that may well be memorable, but where each is only a small part of the bigger picture (see Chapter 7). Consequently, we are left to piece together the bigger picture.

The toolbox

A communications plan. Figure 8.3 sets out a communication plan that we may all have come across. It sets out how we communicate with one another. Such a communication plan usually outlines a schedule, members who are supposed to participate, the communication methods used, and key information covered or received ahead of the communication.

In essence, such communication plans are designed to ensure communication efficiency so that stakeholders are provided with regular, fixed touchpoints for sharing information.

Communication Type	Frequency	Focus
Scrum meeting	Daily	Sharing concerns Tasks for tomorrow ...
Team Meetings	Weekly	Progress update Review of risk register Millstone analysis ...
Status Reports	Weekly	Progress update ...
Quality Assurance Report	Daily	Incident reports ...

Figure 8.3 A typical communication plan.

Emotion-framed messages

Most communication is about sharing information about our progress in continuously managing adversity. This may include reporting the successful completion of tasks or the implementation of decisions. Due to our biases and predispositions, as mentioned earlier, we may attach a positive spin to these communications. Hence, we are apt to repeat them and paint them in more rosy colours, especially those that reach more important, higher-status recipients. In conclusion, we may only convey a picture that corresponds with the emotion we bring to the interaction.

Not listening

Communication (as exemplified in Figure 8.3) may conform to established bureaucratic customs, thereby creating an abundance of information. But in the end, the established, automated form of communication turns into a tick-box exercise, in which communication takes place for its own sake; information is being produced, but it generates no meaning or inspires no commitment to act upon. So, we stop decoding the messages received; we stop listening to them.

Undervaluing and overvaluing

Even if we listen to the abundance of messages, we add to them an emphasis according to how they are conveyed. On one hand, we may overvalue the content of verbal messages that are reinforced by non-verbal cues. On the other, we may undervalue messages that are conveyed in purely written form, as these are less likely to suggest any emotional connotation.

Lack of instantaneous feedback

Written communication is ill-equipped to transmit the nuances of hidden meaning, as it cannot be immediately adjusted to suit the instantaneous judgement of a receiver. Moreover, the sender and receiver may not know how the latter decoded the message without real-time feedback.

Non-flexibility

The lack of instantaneous feedback makes written communication essentially non-flexible; it ends up being concrete and final. Preliminary ideas that may have been discussed verbally, augmented by non-verbal cues, are set in stone, unchangeable, and grow into unmovable and unquestionable expectations and commitments.

Time-consuming

Although we aim to be efficient in communicating, by seeking to transmit so many short, simple, and memorable messages, paradoxically we may end up achieving the opposite. It is time-consuming to encode, send, and decode a message so that message may already be out of date when we receive it and have time to decode it.

Centrifugal wisdom

To make an impact, to hit home with a message in an efficient manner, we are prone to strip it of details, shorten it, simplify it, and repeat it, often in a written form, so it can be documented and memorised. Looking beyond communication as a mere form of transmitting written information to a receiver requires the impetus of personal interaction, a momentum that shapes and forms relationships and activates all our senses, enabling us to code and decode signals of impending adversity (Jahn, Myers and Putnam, 2018).

Therefore, communication needs to be personal, congruent, open, to take place in real-time, caring, and informal. In some circumstances, such as operating a nuclear submarine, this implies an emphasis

> ... on each individual's ownership of the task, responsibility, attention to detail, high professionalism, moral integrity, and mutual respect [which] created the cultural context necessary for high quality communications under high risk and high stress conditions. Communication and recommendations can flow upward from the crewmen to the officers as well as downward. Likewise communication about all kinds of mistakes, operational, technical or administrative, can flow rapidly through the system. Anyone making a mistake can feel free to report it immediately so that the watch officers can really understand what is happening to the system.

> (Bierly and Spender, 1995, p. 651)

High-reliability organisations promote a high-trust culture that breeds openness towards an inconvenient truth that the manifestation of near-misses and accidents is a God-given: that human error is inevitable (Reason, 2008). And yet, despite such inevitability of our shortcomings, we need to do our best to create a shared understanding of what we know and do not know about impending adversity.

In-person communication

Considerable importance is attached to the message, which may be closely scrutinised, and it is the sender of a message who personalises its content and shapes the receiver's willingness to pay attention or commit themselves to act. Communication draws on our senses: on sight to translate personal imagery signals; on sound to transform verbal messaging; on touch to send tactile signals to the brain.

144

If communication is personalised, we become more aware of the feelings and emotions that are attached to a message, resulting in greater empathy with the message and the sender.

Congruence in communication

The clarity in messaging depends on the congruence between verbal and non-verbal communication. Body language, tone of voice, or eye contact need to support the message: if we are trying to convey a positive message, a smile may help, although a grin may look like a signal of overconfidence or amusement.

Scepticism

Personalising verbal messages through emphasising non-verbal aspects of body language, including eye contact, facial expressions, and gestures, may generate empathy with the sender. However, reinforcing commitment to act upon the message is not equivalent to taking the message at face value. We need to allow ourselves to remain sceptical, to express doubt. Consequently, communication requires time and space to critically allow the receiver to feedback on the sender's message. Sender and recipient should treat each other with the necessary respect, without any attempt to undermine the other's competency, rank, and status.

Real-time communication

Whether the sender's message is understood, questioned, or even challenged by sceptical receivers will become apparent from the feedback received. Hence, the message must first be communicated promptly, preferably in real-time so that it is not outdated when the receiver decodes it. Second, feedback should be personal and timely so that the message can be repeatedly re-coded and re-decoded in light of critical feedback to it.

Caring

As receivers of a message, we tend to care about it once we realise that the sender genuinely cares about it, too. Although showing signs of emotion (e.g. stress, concern, and worry) is frowned upon, the signals emitted will show that the message matters personally. With passion and care, we may come to trust each other more and thus be more inclined to speak inconvenient and troublesome truths such as those concerning impending adversity.

Informal interactions

145

A written message is less of an emotive stimulus than one that is conveyed in person. Our tone, voice, and body language open the door to becoming acquainted with another person. In other words, we get to know the sender behind the communicated message.

Freed from all formalities, informal communication can be flexible as it does not need to adhere to fixed timings. It may result in a more cordial relationship and enable real-time feedback. In essence, it provides space for emotional relief, which can be a catalyst for both sender and receiver to air important information concerning worries and concerns that could indicate an impending incident.

Listening

The lack of instant feedback in conventional written communication bothers us as it strips us of an opportunity to reply:

> 'Seek first to understand' involves a very deep shift in paradigm. We typically seek first to be understood. Most people do not listen with the intent to understand; they listen with the intent to reply.

> (Covey, 2004, p. 239)

So, we need to stop talking to ourselves before we can listen to somebody else; creating space, through caring about the message and the messenger, permits us to focus our undivided attention on what is said and what is not said, verbally and non-verbally.

Space to (re)align

The myriad of messages we receive and listen to may quickly overwhelm our capacity to align them (see Chapter 7) to, for example, a bigger picture that sets out the goals for managing impending adversity. Besides focusing on being productive in anticipating and containing impending adversity, we need to set aside some time to zoom-out and align the product of listening to what matters most in our environment.

The toolbox

Grapevine communication. Grapevine communication, a form of informal communication, is best meant for sharing in-person, verbal and non-verbal information in real-time (Davis, 1953; Denning, 2004). Through the grapevine, messages flow in different directions. In principle, one may distinguish between four types of informal networks: single chain, gossip, probability, and cluster (see Figure 8.4).

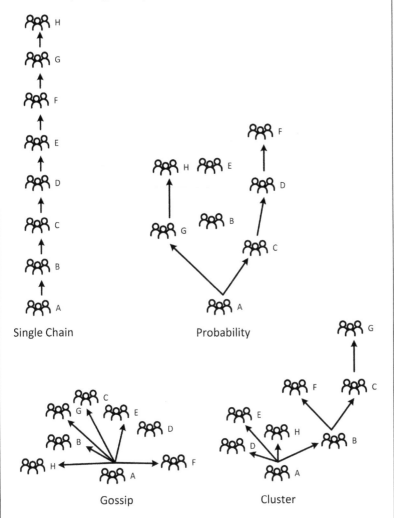

Figure 8.4 Types of informal communication.

Which type or types of formal communication dominate depends on the physical proximity of senders and receivers and their access to technology. If used correctly, any type may enable the rapid coding and decoding of messages – as well as their associated emotions and feelings – that signal an impending incident.

Storytelling. To communicate with each other, we have drawn on stories for centuries. Historically, we have used stories to connect to our cultural and familial traditions, practices, or cultural backdrops. Nowadays, we are surrounded by stories in books, movies, or even news and press releases.

Managerial communication storytelling is not a way of 'talking at' somebody else, but of 'talking with' each other. Key messages may not necessarily stick because they are concise, simple, and repeated over and over again but they can be embedded in a story that provides the decoder with a holistic, authentic, and emotive narrative that we are more likely to listen to.

As presented in Figure 8.5, storytelling follows a dramaturgical structure of exposition, complication, turning point, falling action, and denouncement.

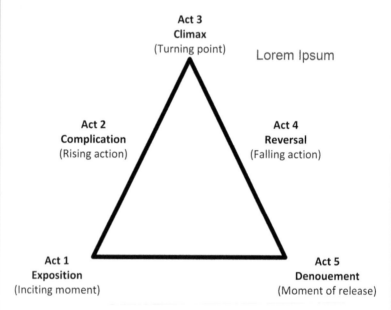

Figure 8.5 Freytag's pyramid (Monarth, 2014, p. 3).

Act 1 sets the scene of the story. We may define the place and time of the story, alluding to a backstory, and draw attention to the main characters. Such scene-setting may relate to past environments in which near-misses or accidents occurred and to the protagonists involved. Act 2 may introduce the practical problem that is associated with a near-miss or accident. It often includes a diagnosis of the problem and the determination of the significance of the impending adversity. The climax (Act 3) provides a period of dramatic tension and ambiguity around the protagonist's actions to deal with impending adversity. Questions of 'Will they be able to deal with it?' will be answered, but not conclusively. The falling action in Act 4 winds down the climactic tensions that were built up. In the context of managing adversity, the protagonists are believed to have dealt successfully with near-misses and accidents in the short term. Still, in fact (or hypothetically), a new problem emerges. The moment of release in Act 5 provides the drama's audience with a conclusion. And yet, in many dramas, a story may raise more questions than it answers.

The dramaturgical structure of a story is one thing; the need to replace centripetal wisdom in communicating is another. In contrast to a predominantly formal, written approach that aims to share information or fragments of information as efficiently as possible, the demands of storytelling are more diverse (see Table 8.1).

Table 8.1 Storytelling

If Your Objective Is:	You Will Need a Story That:	In Telling It, You Will Need to:	Your Story Will Inspire Such Responses as:
Sparking action	Describes how a successful change was implemented in the past, but allows listeners to imagine how it might work in their situation	Avoid excessive detail that will take the audience's mind off its own challenge.	*"Just imagine …"* *"What if …"*
Communicating who you are	Provides audience-engaging drama and reveals some strength or vulnerability from your past.	Include meaningful details, but also make sure the audience has the time and inclination to hear your story.	*"I didn't know that about him!"* *"Now I see what she's driving at."*
Transmitting values	Feels familiar to the audience and prompts discussion about the issues raised by the value being promoted.	Use believable (though perhaps hypothetical) characters and situations, and never forget that the story must be consistent with your own actions.	*"That's so right!"* *"Why don't we do that all the time?"*

(Continued)

If Your Objective Is:	You Will Need a Story That:	In Telling It, You Will Need to:	Your Story Will Inspire Such Responses as:
Fostering collaboration	Movingly recounts a situation that listeners have also experienced and that prompts them to share their own stories about the topic.	Ensure that a set agenda doesn't squelch this swapping of stories – and that you have an action plan ready to tap the energy unleashed by this narrative chain reaction.	*"That reminds me of the time that I ..."* *"Hey, I've got a story like that."*
Taming the grapevine	Highlights, often through the use of gentle humour, some aspect of a rumour that reveals it to be untrue or unlikely.	Avoid the temptation to be mean-spirited, and be sure that the rumour is indeed false.	*"No kidding!"* *"I'd never thought about it like that before!"*
Sharing knowledge	Focuses on mistakes made and shows in some detail how they were corrected, with an explanation of why the solution worked.	Solicit alternative – and possibly better – solutions.	*"There but for the grace of God ..."* *"Wow! We'd better watch that from now on."*
Leading people into the future	Evokes the future you want to create without providing excessive detail that will only turn out to be wrong.	Be sure of your storytelling skills. (Otherwise, use a story in which the past can serve as a springboard to the future.)	*"When do we start?"* *"Let's do it!"*

Source: Denning, 2004, p. 127.

Visual communication. In the novel 'Fathers and Sons' (1862), the Russian author Ivan Turgenev said that *"The drawing shows me at a glance what would be spread over ten pages in a book".* What is now expressed as *"A picture is worth a thousand words"* supports the idea of visual communication. Visual communication encompasses charts, presentations, graphs, figures, posters, timelines, mind maps, or simply images.

The use of visual communication varies; it is often used to supplement and augment the written or spoken word. In principle, the visualisation of communication grabs more attention (as in Figure 8.6), gives more meaning, evokes a greater emotive stimulus, and, most importantly, conveys a greater breadth and depth of discriminatory meaning.

Figure 8.6 An image.

Communicating - Revisiting the Bhopal gas tragedy

In 1969, Union Carbide India Limited (UCIL) established a production line for the pesticide Sevin in the Indian city of Bhopal, home to a population of 800,000. The pesticide relied on methyl isocyanate (MIC) as an intermediate. On its own, this reactant is extremely toxic. Therefore, in 1979, three underground storage tanks were constructed, holding 68 tonnes of MIC.

The plant was plagued by a series of near-misses as well as accidents. For example, in August 1982, a plant worker, who was not ordered to wear protective equipment, came into contact with liquid MIC and suffered burns to 30% of his body.

In the months leading to the disaster, constant problems with pressurising the underground tanks resulted in a partial shutdown of the MIC production plant. The MIC-related safety systems failed; one of the underground tanks held 42 tonnes of MIC, whereas only 30 tonnes is considered safe.

On the evening of 2 December 1984, it is believed that water entered the tank via a side pipe. It triggered an exothermic reaction that ruptured the tank. About 30 tonnes of MIC turned into a deadly cloud that was blown over the city of Bhopal. On the following morning, the city's inhabitants experienced breathlessness, stomach pains, and vomiting. Panic set in. Those who inhaled a larger amount of the gas were killed instantly.

As the plant was closed to outsiders, the government's response was to hide information from the public:

> The confusion was not just about the identity of the gas that had leaked that night. The state government's posture following the leak was astonishing. The authorities withheld vital information about the effects of the gas on human beings, birds, animals and vegetables. All investigative findings were kept away from doctors and scientists and no guidelines for treatment were available. The wind direction data was also not made public. The government repeatedly assured the people that air, water and vegetation were safe for consumption.

(Shastri, 2020, p. 35)

The death toll from the Bhopal gas tragedy is estimated to be around 15,000 with 200,000–300,000 inhabitants suffering short and long-term health effects. It was one of the worst industrial accidents in modern history.

Just-this-way and just-for-now

Typically, our professional environment is defined by bureaucratic information processing. Information is communicated in written form, objectified and analysed to limit and contain any adversity within the organisation. Despite the advantages of efficiency, consistency, and transparency that come with bureaucratised communication (Jannis, 2011), this also hampers our ability to communicate openly with each other about the prevention of near-misses and the containment of accidents.

It is therefore no surprise that closed communication, in the form of brief, formal, written, and remote messages, is deemed the single best way to anticipate and respond to the threat of an impending incident. In the wake of the release of the toxic gas at UCIL's plant, little information was provided concerning the impending disastrous effects on the population of Bhopal. The reason for not openly sharing that information was the local government's inability to grasp the extent and nature of unfolding disaster. Even more significant was the just-this-way (see Figure 8.7) hidden agenda of UCIL which was a driving factor in attempting to ignore, downplay, and thus avoid, accountability and responsibility for containing the rapidly worsening situation.

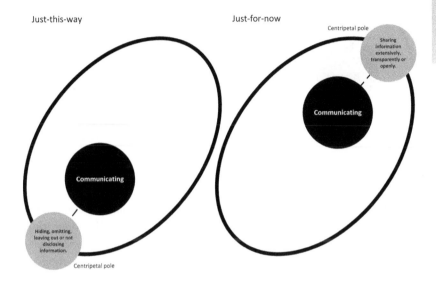

Figure 8.7 Just-this-way and just-for-now polarity (communicating).

Just-for-now, let's go through a parallel scenario in which information was shared extensively, transparently, and openly. The local population of Bhopal would have been bombarded with a myriad of information, a plethora of messages around every detail of the accident, its effect, and the response to it. Given that no definitive single scenario was available at the moment of the accident, the local emergency services would have to be prepared and ready to engage with unprocessed and unfiltered information. The result could have been as confusing and chaotic as if there had been overuse of the centripetal pole of communication.

Just-in-case and just-in-time

How we move away from an either/or best option to an integrated third way of communication is again defined by looking at just-in-case and just-in-time perspectives, focusing on the synthesis of both poles and the benefits such integration generates (see Figure 8.8).

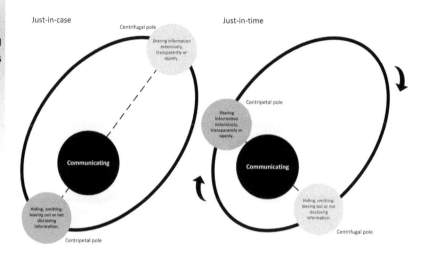

Figure 8.8 Just-in-case and just-in-time polarity (communicating).

The hiding, leaving out, or not disclosing information pole makes us think about what information is sufficiently relevant to require being turned into messages that can be transmitted efficiently, and with maximum effect. The opposite pole enables the receivers of information to process it by themselves, filtering out 'white noise' from information that the receiver deems relevant. Hence, the receiver can be more discriminatory about which details to take note of (see Chapter 4) and which specifics to discard.

To operationalise just-in-case and just-in-time thinking on communication, the following principles may be informative and instructive:

JUST-IN-CASE, we long for listening to the message WHILE paying attention to the messenger's emotions. The message that signals an impending incident is essential; so is the personalised sender and receiver of a message. We need to have faith in the other person, his or her intention and credibility, rather than stopping to be critical about the message's content.

Open communication, appealing to emotions, may reveal concerns and worries that indicate an impending incident. Besides, it generates greater emotional or affective commitment to preventing an incident or containing its consequences. In other words, it is 'easier' to be non-committal to the written word than to a message that is conveyed in an emotive, caring, and passionate manner.

JUST-IN-CASE, we aim for reason-based, goal-oriented messages WHILE craving stories. Although we may not have had the time to relentlessly tell stories, we should still be reluctant to spew out messages that are not tailored to an audience, a goal or objective, or a bigger picture that others draw on to align themselves (see Chapter 7) with us or others.

JUST-IN-CASE, we promote the use of official, formal communication channels WHILE encouraging people to engage on a personal level informally. Informal channels of communication that result in questionable and unreasonable rumours and gossip should be discouraged. Some checkpoints of verification of the communication's credibility should be implemented to maintain trust. Encourage people not to leave any communication untouched; allow and incentivise critical feedback.

JUST-IN-TIME, we long for listening to the message WHILE paying attention to the messenger's emotions, AS LONG AS we do not cognitively overload the receiver. The creation of open, in-person communication for its own sake may result in information overload. Hand in hand with fostering open communication is the need to enhance our ability to process it. Hence, processing capabilities need to be established that decode, record, store, and most importantly, process feedback summaries and synthesise the information for us. Nevertheless, we can only continue to do this for as long as communication is not excessive. We must not overload our personal devices and communication inboxes to such an extent that our capacity to turn raw data into meaning is exceeded.

Towards a paradox mindset

Looking through the lens of a paradox, we may conclude that no matter how we balance open and closed communication or whatever integrative option we may come up with, we always arrive at the same result. Paradoxically speaking, a solution to resolve the complementary tensions between open and closed communication may become untenable. What is your third way to exploit the benefits (while avoiding the detrimental effects) of these tensions around the important construct of communicating?

References

Bierly, P. and Spender, J. C. (1995) 'Culture and high reliability organizations: The case of the nuclear submarine', *Journal of Management*, 21(4), pp. 639–656.

Covey, S. R. (2004) *7 habits of highly effective people*. New York: Free Press.

Davis, K. (1953) 'Management communication and the grapevine', *Harvard Business Review*, 31(5), pp. 43–49.

Denning, S. (2004) 'Telling tales', *Harvard Business Review*, 82(5), pp. 122–129.

Fazio, L. K. *et al.* (2015) 'Knowledge does not protect against illusory truth', *Journal of Experimental Psychology: General*, 144(5), pp. 993–1002.

Jahn, J. L. S., Myers, K. K. and Putnam, L. L. (2018) 'Metaphors of communication in high reliability organizations', in Ramanujam, R. and Roberts, K. H. (eds.) *Organizing for reliability: A guide for research and practice.* Stanford, CA: Stanford University Press, pp. 169–193.

James N. D. (2001). Evaluating framing effects. *Journal of Economic Psychology*, *22*(1), pp. 91–101.

Jannis, K. (2011) 'Bureaucracy under Siege: On information, collaboration, and networks', in Clegg, S., Harris, M., and Höpfl, H. (eds.) *Managing modernity: Beyond bureaucracy?* Oxford: Oxford University Press, pp. 130–153.

Levine, T. R. (2014) 'Truth-Default Theory (TDT)', *Journal of Language and Social Psychology*, 33(4), pp. 378–392.

Monarth, H. (2014) 'The irresistible power of storytelling as a strategic business tool', *Harvard Business School Review, March*, pp. 250–256.

Reason, J. (2008) *The human contribution: Unsafe acts, accidents and heroic recoveries.* Boca Raton, FL: Taylor & Francis.

Rogers, C. R. and Roethlisberger, J. (1952) 'Barriers and gateways to communication', *Harvard Business Review*, 69(6), pp. 105–111.

Shastri, L. (2020) *Bhopal disaster: An eyewitness account.* Bhopal: Writers' Dream Publications.

Chapter 9

Deferring to others

How successfully we anticipate and respond to near-misses and accidents depends on whether we submit to an expert opinion associated with an extensive skill set, knowledge base and experience, or trust somebody in recognition of their authority in the perceived absence of expertise.

Deferring to somebody else by delegation or escalation (see Chapter 6), submitting to a checklist (see Chapter 5), or trusting somebody's expertise poses a challenge. But, in principle, taking expertise into account is central to most of the unconventional, centrifugal pearls of wisdom mentioned so far.

Just as it is commendable to rely on our expertise and the expertise all around us, it is also easy to discount it in anticipating and responding to near-misses and accidents:

> Expertise can be ignored ... dismissed because of its presumed logic, conditioned by rank, minimised because of self-interest, or rendered secondary by prevailing routines.

> (Weick and Sutcliffe, 2015, p. 114)

As shown in Figure 9.1, we tend to accept a deficiency in expertise and competence and defer to authority. You may argue that this is already covered in Chapter 6. Yes and no; Chapter 6 addressed a struggle over the ability to influence. Suppose we cannot influence, prevent, or contain impending and materialising adversity. In that case, we may have to develop an integrative way to both escalate it away from us and own it until a worsening situation is brought back under control.

This construct of deferring is closely aligned with the one of influence, but it focuses more on the question of how to influence: by counting on one's competency or yielding (without submitting) to additional expertise, knowledge, ideas, or opinions.

157

DOI: 10.4324/9781003083115-9

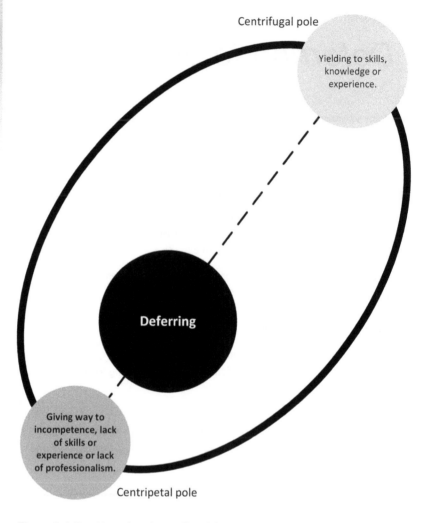

Centrifugal pole

Yielding to skills,
knowledge or
experience.

Deferring

Giving way to
incompetence, lack
of skills or
experience or lack
of professionalism.

Centripetal pole

Figure 9.1 Centripetal and centrifugal forces (deferring).

Centripetal wisdom

When faced with the failure to anticipate and contain the ramifications of near-misses and accidents, we tend to question our own influence (see Chapter 6), but are more likely to question and dismiss other people's experience and the associated level of expertise and proficiency connected to such failure.

That is to say that our acknowledgement of our own and other's perceived managerial imperfections is not compensated for by our longing to iron them out but instead is superseded by a higher force that is defined less by expertise than by rank, or status, or the authority of a rulebook to which we are made compliant (see Chapter 5).

Therefore (see Figure 9.2), we may at first not defer to somebody else's expertise due to our egocentric tendencies to believe that we are superior in anticipating and responding to incidents. Then, our perceptions of other people's lack of expertise and proficiency reinforces our tendency to submit – to defer to somebody else's rank or status or the authority of a rule, process, or procedure (see Chapter 5), or abdicate our responsibility altogether through an escalation process (see Chapter 6).

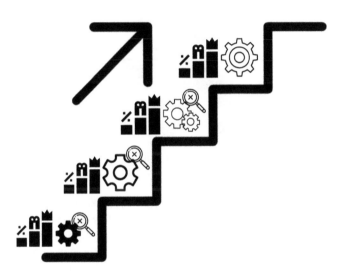

Figure 9.2 Deference to rank, status, authority, rules, processes, and procedures.

Our preferences for and inclinations towards deferring to a higher authority – its power to command, its thought, opinion, or even behaviours – are augmented by biases such as authority and hindsight bias and the bandwagon effect:

Authority. The consistent process of adhering to a regimen may be reinforced by authority, rank, and status. In other words, authority, rank, and status are relied upon to hammer home the need to adhere rigidly to a rulebook. As we have a deep-seated duty to authority, we tend to comply (Milgram, 2009).

Bandwagon. The bandwagon effect is very influential in combination with authority bias (Myers, Wojcicki, and Aardema, 1977). We tend to conform to certain behaviours, beliefs, attitudes, or ideas because everyone else, especially those with rank, status, and a position of authority, adopts and sanctions them.

The toolbox

Hierarchy. In organisations, we tend to establish hierarchical structures to improve the effectiveness of tasks carried out. Hierarchical levels of operational, middle management, and top-level management (see Figure 9.3) define authority, power, and responsibilities to facilitate accountability and communication (see Chapter 8) and determine clear career paths for us.

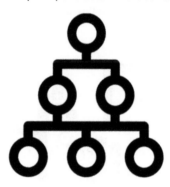

Figure 9.3 Principle hierarchical structure.

Often, within this structure, a top-down decision-making process prevails. Top-level management tends to distinguish itself by rank, status, authority, power, responsibility, and expertise. Strategic decisions are then broken down in a Taylorist manner, occasionally in the form of to-do lists (see Chapter 7) to guide lower-ranked subordinates in their daily task orientation.

The resulting chain of command, the route by which instructions and communications flow, provides a range of benefits. Responsibilities and accountability for task execution are clearly assigned, both for those who define the task at the top and those who carry it out at the bottom of the hierarchy. Clear reporting channels have defined both ways to enable efficient communication and reporting.

Submission

Even though we tend to believe we know better, we are prone to give way to something – a rule, routine, procedures, or individual – defined by rank, status, or authority. This does not per se constitute a state of resignation, rather it is deference to a superior but ultimately deceptive 'truth' that is anything but informed by expertise.

Such submission may go hand in hand with the perception of being no more than a cog in a wheel (see Chapter 5) so that any commitment to own a problem until it is resolved is eroded:

> Deference to authority is deeply engrained in most societies, so it's no wonder that it also shows up in many organisations. We honor our parents and are taught to obey them. We're similarly encouraged to respect our teachers, elders, community, and religious leaders. Given all of this cultural reinforcement, pushing back against hierarchical authority often goes against the grain. It's made even more difficult in organisations when such push-back is implicitly (or explicitly) discouraged — either by an unwillingness of senior people to receive feedback or subtle punishment for people who speak up.
>
> (Ashkenas, 2011)

Lack of distinction

Too great an emphasis on rank, status, and authority may make the true location of expertise hard to see. In hierarchically run organisations, we tend to equate authority, rank, and status with expertise (Weick and Sutcliffe, 2007). In extreme cases, near-misses and accidents travel through a hierarchical system, from authority to authority, each of them lacking the sensitivity, self-awareness, and commitment to engage with near-misses and accidents.

Self-importance

Being equipped with rank, status, and authority may well make us feel important and we may radiate an aura of all-knowing:

> …if other people assume that you are all-knowing, then they won't take the trouble to tell you what they know since they assume that you already know it. Sometimes people who are lower in a hierarchy fail to raise questions or act on their concerns out of fear – fear of repercussions or fear of stepping on someone's toes.
>
> (Weick and Sutcliffe, 2015, p. 127)

Top-heavy

The concentration of expertise in higher echelons of an organisation is intensified by the lure of vertical promotions, bringing a change not only in salary and responsibility but also in status and authority. Thus, it is not surprising that many organisational hierarchies are top-heavy with expertise. At the operational level, though, people who have been promoted out of that level are replaced with less familiar newcomers, less ready, and less prepared to anticipate and respond to near-misses and accidents. In fact, they are more prone to submit to already established authority, rank, and status.

Silo mentality

Our egocentric tendencies, reinforced by rank, status, and authority fortify a silo mentality and result in an unwillingness to share data or knowledge and encourage the open free flow of information (see Chapter 8). Ultimately, the prospect of amassing authority, rank, and status, possibly through vertical promotions, feeds the competitive nature of resilient organising. However, competition becomes detrimental if it drives single-handed actions undertaken regardless of consequences and at the expense of others (see Chapter 7).

Bureaucracy

Hierarchical organising, in particular in bigger organisations, requires multi-layered systems and processes (see Chapter 5) to maintain uniformity, conformity, consistency, and control (see Chapter 6). In many cases, though, it creates redundancies (which are ill-equipped to anticipate and respond to near-misses and accidents), arbitrariness and, subsequently, inefficiencies.

Centripetal wisdom

Whereas, conventionally, we may be resigned to perceptions of incompetence or the lack of professional behaviour in the face of near-misses and accidents, in submitting to hierarchical structures and bureaucratic impulses to conform and comply, we may unexpectedly yield to expertise. In a high-reliability organisation,

> Deference to expertise includes a pattern of respectful yielding, domain-specific knowledge, compressed and generalisable experience, and relative expertise ...

(Weick and Sutcliffe, 2007, p. 116)

If we comply with the need to own a near-miss and/or accident (see Chapter 6), we can allow expertise to inform, to challenge, to guide, and to question our decision-making without abdicating authority or seeking absolution through escalations based on the excuse of rank, status, and hierarchical structures.

In essence, referring to Chapter 6, the buck can only stop anywhere if we own misses and accidents and manage them in the most informed manner by relying on the wisdom and expertise of not just of ourselves, but multiple internal or external experts (see Chapter 10).

Experience building

Our reliance on hindsight (see Chapter 3) may simply urge us to operate within the comfort zone of what we have experienced in the past as a predictor for present and future actions. In such circumstances, becoming an expert is largely about:

> … improving the skills you already have and extending the reach and range of your skills. The enormous concentration required to undertake these twin tasks limits the amount of time you can spend doing them. The famous violinist Nathan Milstein wrote: 'Practice as much as you feel you can accomplish with concentration. Once when I became concerned because others around me practiced all day long, I asked [my mentor] Professor Auer how many hours I should practice, and he said, "It really doesn't matter how long. If you practice with your fingers, no amount is enough. If you practice with your head, two hours is plenty."
>
> (Ericsson, Prietula, and Cokely, 2007, p. 119)

This implies that we as experts should not just emphasise experiencing the same or similar near-misses and accidents in a domain-specific (Weick and Sutcliffe, 2007) environment for the purpose of dealing with the same or similar aspect of adversity better; instead, we should widen our horizons beyond past experiences and stretch our minds (see Chapter 5) into the reality of the not yet experienced.

Expertise sharing and retention

Expertise is always at risk: It may be routinised (see Chapter 5) and thus not challenged and updated; it may depart and be forgotten with the migration or departure of authority, rank, or status. To retain expertise where it matters (see Chapter 10), the accumulation of rank, status, and authority, through, for example, promoting experts to the upper echelons of a hierarchy, should be questioned. Instead of equating rank, status, and authority with financial well-being, we could appeal to other basic needs in order to retain our expertise where it matters, which is not necessarily at the top of the hierarchy.

Migration of decision-making power

The previous argument for accumulating, expanding, and retaining expertise at the lower levels may be as foolish as concentrating it at the top:

> Identify pockets of expertise before you need them. Don't assume the expertise is at the top and disappears as you go down the hierarchy. When problems occur, let decision making migrate to people who have the most expertise to deal with the problem.

(Weick and Sutcliffe, 2007, p. 126)

Humility

We may feel more self-important if we push our expertise through an organisation and force our opinionated rights and wrongs on others. Nevertheless, being an expert does not include providing somebody else in need with the 'right' answers, but is more about asking the 'right' questions, raising the 'right' challenges to somebody else's assumptions (see Chapter 4). As experts, we are only useful insofar as we are humble enough to acknowledge our limits through the continuous questioning and challenging of our own and other people's expertise.

Breaking down barriers

Under the cloak of rank, status, and authority, a silo mentality emerges which must be broken down or softened by aligning ourselves with each other (see Chapter 7). In other words, we must grow our understanding of each other and be sensitive to how (often) we interact so that we get to know each other's contributions to managing near-misses and accidents, as well as the tensions that can arise in coordination and collaboration across hierarchical boundaries. An open and honest communication (see Chapter 8) is central to such heedful interrelating (Weick and Roberts, 1993).

The toolbox

Unconventional wisdom, as previously outlined, gravitates towards deference to a higher authority that is not necessarily grounded in expertise. There is, therefore, a need for experience building to help us avoid giving way to the primary temptation to defer to a higher authority. Experience building should underscore the safe encounter with 'new' adversity (see Chapter 3) before it materialises and share that experience in order to widen our own and others' horizon.

Simulations, games, and role plays. In Chapter 3, tools and techniques such as scenario planning, horizon scanning, and a pre-mortem were suggested as means to widen our horizons about alternative scenarios beyond past-informed experiences. But because these mostly operate through our conceptual minds – through listening, reading, and discussing – they lack experiential power.

Simulations, games, and role-plays are cost-effective methods of responding to the need to experience alternative futures in order to enhance our expertise in anticipating and responding to near-misses and accidents. The boundaries of our expertise are most likely expanded but also questioned and challenged when we experience the consequences of our actions in a safe environment. We repeat these experiences in different, preferably extreme scenarios to stretch (see Chapter 5) our thinking and gain expertise from them.

Informal networks. The diffusion of experiences and expertise may unfold in an informal manner through grapevine communication and storytelling (see Chapter 8). As we are social beings, we tend to form networks comprising colleagues, friends, superiors, subordinates, and those we have worked closely with. These informal networks are not defined by hierarchical structures but emerge over time (see Figure 9.4).

Figure 9.4 Informal network.

Informal networks are a major source of news and can mature into networks that render the location of expertise visible and accessible, as we focus less on rank, status, and authority in more mundane situations, such as having a coffee or tea together during a break.

A more formalised way of sharing expertise is the setting up of a 'campfire':

> This is a convened meeting of less experienced individuals or a mixture of experts and others in which experts present lessons, then discuss and expand on them, generating new knowledge.

> (Leonard and Martin, 2019, p. 3)

The degree of informality contributes to the extent to which barriers of rank, status, and authority can be broken down to the lowest levels in a hierarchy, as individuals, with all their imperfections and fallibilities, have their chance to shine. Their imperfections should not be interpreted as incompetence or be used to disrespect the experiences and expertise of the individuals we informally engage with.

Deferring - Revisiting the Black Death

In October 1347, 12 ships from the Black Sea arrived at the Sicilian port of Messina. Boarding the ship, the dockworkers gasped at the horrors they had to witness. The majority of the ship's crew was dead, and those still barely alive were covered in back boils, seeping blood and pus. The Sicilian authorities swiftly ordered the ships to leave the harbour, but it was too late to halt the transmission of what became known as the Black Death (also referred to as bubonic, pneumonic, and septicaemic plague. It is estimated that there were between 75 and 200 million deaths/casualties in Eurasia alone.

At the onset of one of the biggest catastrophes in human history, rumours of a terrible plague swept the European kingdoms and empires. As there was close to no medical knowledge about the plague, plague doctors (later identifiable in some cases by their bird-like 'beak' masks) reverted to crude and unsophisticated treatments that they believed had helped them with other ailments and illnesses: bleeding and leeches, drinking their own urine or using herbs and flowers.

People continued to die in their thousands; subsequently, they deferred to a higher power as these treatments failed to have the necessary effect. Many believed it was God's wrath that had come upon them, punishing them for their sins of greed, blasphemy, or worldliness. Others assumed that the beauty of young girls attracted the Black Death:

> In the Palm Sunday procession many fainted with ecstasy or with sheer terror of the horrors that surely awaited them. Despite the fears of contagion which wracked the community, it was the largest such assembly that could be remembered. So great were the crowds walking behind the cross that the procession was slowed almost to a halt as it squeezed itself between the houses and hedges in the narrow parts of the road which led from the church up Jolycote Hill. Everyone clutched palms of yew, box and willow that had been blessed by the priests, and at the end of the day they carried them home to serve as charms to protect their houses against the plague.

(Hatcher, 2010, p. 157)

Just-this-way and just-for-now

By default, the management of near-misses and accidents is clouded and obscured by our lack of, or incomplete, knowledge about impending adversity and our incomplete expertise in anticipating and containing it. It is unsurprising that, in light of our fallibility (see Chapter 6), we gravitate towards resignation to a higher authority (see Figure 9.5).

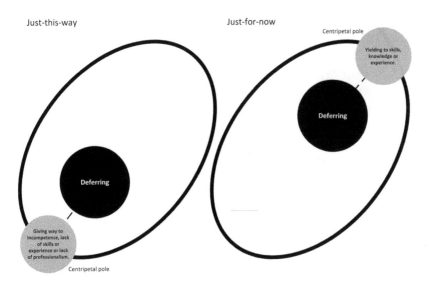

Figure 9.5 Just-this-way and just-for-now polarity (deferring).

Just-this-way, as during the Black Death, the majority of people deferred to belief in and reverence for God, so may we defer to the higher, superseding authority of rank and status in more contemporary managerial environments. This deference provides greater comfort and straightforward answers to a predicament.

Pivoting to the other extreme, people may eventually have yielded to skills, knowledge, and experience that were scarce at the beginning of the Back Death. Although efforts to contain the spread of the plague through quarantining were made, there would have been blind reliance on the expert, the Plague Doctor, too.

Just-in-case and just-in-time

With reference to deferring, overreliance on either pole appears disadvantageous, so we need to aim for a third way that epitomises both/and interpretation (see Figure 9.6), but only if these extreme poles can yield some benefits. Resignation to incompetence, lack of skills and experience or lack of professionalism may be converted into the need to gather more knowledge, to challenge our own assumptions, making us ask for help.

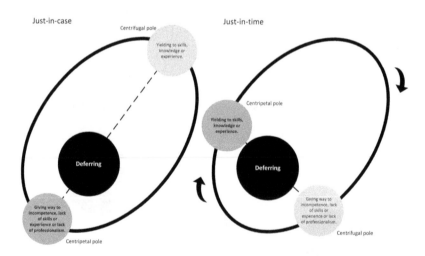

Figure 9.6 Just-in-case and just-in-time polarity (deferring).

Integrating these benefits with the opposite pole means not submitting to somebody's else knowledge or giving up and giving in to an easy way out through escalations (see Chapter 6), but points to a third way that results in neither total resignation nor outright submission. Instead, both/and principles harness the good of both poles and limit the detrimental effects of overuse of either/or polarity.

JUST-IN-CASE, we listen to a higher authority WHILE being reluctant to follow it. Seeing the lack of competence around us may make us feel like giving up and submitting to a higher authority that is equipped with more power, rank and status. Nevertheless, it is a just-in-case guiding principle that we can listen to a higher authority while actively questioning and challenging it:

> Hierarchical organisations seduce us with psychological rewards like feelings of power and status. What's more, multilevel hierarchies remain the best available mechanism for doing complex work. It is unrealistic to expect that we will do away with them in the foreseeable future. It seems more sensible to accept the reality that hierarchies are here to stay and work hard to reduce their highly noxious byproducts, while making them more habitable for humans and more productive as well.
>
> (Leavitt, 2003, p. 102)

JUST-IN-CASE, we aspire to widen and deepen our expertise WHILE we continue to show humility about it:

> When we begin to identify as experts, our outlook can narrow, both in daily work and in times of crisis. We become reluctant to admit mistakes and failings, thus hindering our development. We distance ourselves from those 'beneath' us, making it harder to earn their affection and trust. And as the dynamics of our businesses change, we risk being bypassed or replaced by colleagues on the rise, outsiders adept at learning new things, or artificial intelligence algorithms that can perform rote tasks faster and better than we can. Over time the very expertise that led to our success can leave us feeling unhappy, unsatisfied, and stuck.
>
> (Finkelstein, 2019, p. 154)

While not permitting our egos to tell us that we are the only expert in the room, we should have confidence in what we know about anticipating and containing the fallout of near-misses and accidents while always seeking additional expertise to listen to.

JUST-IN-CASE, we build up expertise where it matters WHILE allowing expertise to settle in the higher echelons of a hierarchy. To manage impending adversity well, we need to allow for vertical promotions. Promoting expertise away from the operational level of an organisation, though, leaves a void. We should try to protect and build up expertise where it matters – at the frontline – while keeping the door open for us to progress up the hierarchy (see Chapter 10).

To add a dynamic dimension to the guiding just-in-case principles, let's expand and broaden on the first principle:

JUST-IN-TIME, we listen to a higher authority WHILE being reluctant to follow it, as long as we think we can influence the management of adversity. With reference to Chapter 6, we keep a tab on how influential we are and only own the management of impending adversity as long as we think we are capable of actively managing it.

Towards a paradox mindset

> The yielding is respectful because participants in HROs know the limits of their own knowledge and experience. They seldom 'mistake the change of a feeling of doubt into a feeling of assurance as knowledge' (Bacon, 2012, p. 54). On the one hand experts know what they don't know. They know the gaps in their own knowledge (Leonard-Barton and Swap, 2005, p. 57). Novices, on the other hand, 'have little idea of what is even included in the particular knowledge domain.' This means that deference is triggered in the context of relative expertise.

> (Adapted from Weick and Sutcliffe, 2015, p. 116)

As novices, lacking the experience and expertise to anticipate near-miss incidents and accidents efficiently, we may defer more readily to a higher authority than to a so-called expert. On the other hand, yielding to an expert may box in our thinking. Ultimately, as with the previous processes covered in this book, it is a question of both/and. The answer is the definition of guiding just-in-case principles that are to be applied dynamically here-and-now.

References

Ashkenas, R. (2011) *The dangers of deference, Harvard Business Review*. Available at: https://hbr.org/2011/07/the-dangers-of-deference.

Bacon, M. (2012) *Pragmatism*. Malden, MA: Polity Press.

Ericsson, K. A., Prietula, M. J. and Cokely, E. T. (2007) 'The making of an expert', *Harvard Business Review*, 85(7/8), p. 114.

Finkelstein, S. (2019) 'Don't be blinded by your own expertise', *Harvard Business Review*, 97(3), pp. 153–158.

Hatcher, J. (2010) *The Black Death: An intimate history*. London: Orion.

Leavitt, H. J. (2003) 'Why hierarchies thrive', *Harvard Business Review*, 81(3), pp. 96–112.

Leonard, D. and Martin, J. (2019) 'How your organization's experts can share their knowledge', *Harvard Business Review*. https://hbr.org/2019/12/how-your-organizations-experts-can-share-their-knowledge

Leonard-Barton, D. and Swap, W. C. (2005) *Deep smarts: How to cultivate and transfer enduring business wisdom*. Camebridge, MA: Harvard Business School Press.

Milgram, S. (2009) *Obedience to authority: An experimental view*. New York: HarperCollins.

Myers, D. G., Wojcicki, S. B. and Aardema, B. S. (1977) 'Attitude comparison: Is there ever a Bandwagon effect?', *Journal of Applied Social Psychology*, 7(4), pp. 341–347.

Weick, K. and Roberts, K. (1993) 'Collective mind in organizations: Heedful interrelating on flight decks', *Administrative Science Quarterly*, 38(3), p. 357.

Weick, K. and Sutcliffe, K. (2007) *Managing the unexpected: Resilient performance in an age of uncertainty*. 2nd edn. San Francisco, CA: Jossey Bass.

Weick, K. and Sutcliffe, K. (2015) *Managing the unexpected: Sustained performance in a complex world*. 3rd edn. Hoboken, NJ: Wiley.

Chapter 10

Accessing resources

The previous two chapters focused on the boundaries surrounding our influence and what it means to cross these boundaries by deferring to others. This chapter focuses on the related challenge of accessing and considers the bipolar alternative of either accessing external support or becoming reliant on already established internal assistance, backing, or guidance (see Figure 10.1).

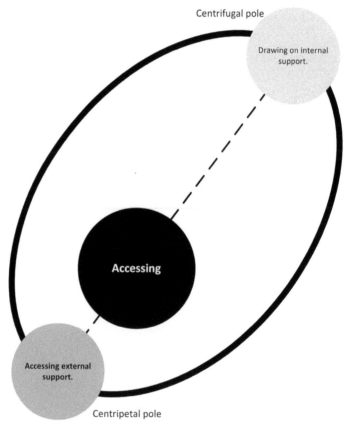

Figure 10.1 Centripetal and centrifugal forces (accessing).

DOI: 10.4324/9781003083115-10

A resource may include materials, finances, technology, equipment, or other people's expertise, anything that is necessary to anticipate and contain materialising adversity. In this chapter, the focus is exclusively on us, the human resource, as the key enabler of mindful behaviour.

The challenge is that when we feel overburdened by the task of anticipating and containing an impending crisis (see Chapter 6), we may be tempted to call in some additional human resources (see Figure 10.2) rather than investing in, developing and expanding our in-house capacity.

Figure 10.2 A question of external support.

Centripetal wisdom

Despite our egocentric inclinations to overestimate our internal capabilities and capacities to anticipate and contain the consequences of near-miss incidents and accidents, we are often pushed to our limits (see Chapters 6 and 9), which makes us consider bringing in external support. The biases, inclinations, and preferences described below compound such a desire to externalise our management of adversity. In addition to those already mentioned in previous chapters, the following are noteworthy:

Sunk cost fallacy. In combination with the status quo bias (Samuelson and Zeckhauser, 1988; Kahneman and Tversky, 1991), the sunk cost fallacy may make us choose an option that preserves the status quo and is perceived as least risky. If we have invested considerable time and effort in building up an internal repository of skills and capabilities, we may decide to ringfence those internal capabilities and opt for additional external ones.

Availability heuristics. We are deceived by the tendency to draw on information that is easily accessible and comes to mind quickly and easily (Kahneman and Lovallo, 2003). Acknowledging near-misses and accidents as failures to prevent such occurrences, we are inclined to jump to the conclusion that our internal capacities and capabilities are not sufficient. Even if we are primed towards self-importance and over-optimism, our default position is to keep open our option to rely on external support (see Chapters 6 and 9).

Hyperbolic discounting. Under pressure, we may fall prey to hyperbolic discounting; rewarding immediate gains more favourably than long-term successes (Ainslie and Haslam, 1992).

A combination of the sunk cost fallacy and status quo bias could make us predisposed to lean on external support as a quick fix to address resource constraints (see Figure 10.3).

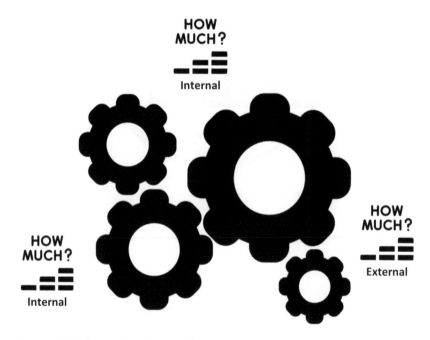

Figure 10.3 A question of capacity.

The main benefits of accessing external resources are lower operational and labour costs. In addition, external resources can be deployed and replaced much more quickly. In principle, external resources allow us to develop greater robustness by dynamically adjusting the resource base necessary to engage with impending adversity.

The toolbox

Outsourcing and lean thinking. The process of outsourcing follows a strategic decision to increase efficiency by hiring external capacities and capabilities to perform tasks or provide services. Typically, non-core competencies are outsourced so that greater priority can be placed on the remaining core functions, processes, or service delivery.

In that respect, the idea of leanness is rooted in the principle of creating value with less waste. The five principles of Lean are:

1. Specify value from the standpoint of the end customer.
2. Identify all the steps in the value stream, eliminating whenever possible those steps that do not create value.
3. Make the value-creating steps occur in tight sequence so the product will flow smoothly towards the customer.
4. As flow is introduced, let customers pull value from the next upstream activity.
5. As value is specified, identify value streams, remove wasted steps, and introduce flow and pull, repeating this process and continuing it until a state of perfection is reached in which perfect value is created with no waste. (Adapted from Project Management Institute, 2022)

So, in principle, core processes, functions, and services are not to be outsourced.

Outsourcing processes and lean thinking have been elevated to a lean enterprise philosophy, with a key emphasis on reducing waste and seemingly unnecessary system redundancies in resources, time, energy, and effort:

> A concerted effort by companies across the industrial landscape to embrace the lean enterprise and find new tasks for excess employees will be vastly superior to any industrial policy that governments devise. An economy dominated by lean enterprises continually trying to improve their productivity, flexibility, and customer responsiveness might finally be able to avoid the kind of social upheavals that have occurred when new production systems have rendered existing ones obsolete.

> If this sea change in industrial practice comes to pass, most individuals, companies, and enterprises will prosper. Equally important, we will witness a productivity explosion, coupled with employment stability, that will provide the long-sought antidote to the economic stagnation plaguing all advanced economies.

(Womack and Jones, 1994, p. 103)

Denominator management

A major disadvantage of the outsourcing practice is that we are inclined to focus our attention on mere cost reductions rather than on value creation or the protection of value through high-reliability management:

> It [outsourcing] focuses on the supply side, not the demand side. And because it occupies substantial management resources and executive time, it can unwittingly become another form of denominator management rather than revenue creation – not a prescription for long-term success.
>
> (Earl, 1996, p. 27)

Emotional and structural detachment

Although greater external support helps us to provide greater supply flexibility, such capacities are emotionally and structurally detached (at least at the point at which these capacities are first parachuted in) from the context in which adversity occurs and from the people who are supposed to own adversity until it is resolved. Just imagine what it is like to be this outsourced capacity, belonging to another, detached organisational entity. We may show less empathy and less commitment to anticipating and containing near-misses and accidents; in the end, they do not affect us because we are outsourced skills and capabilities.

More formality, less familiarity

External human resources may be accustomed to different norms, rules, procedures, and working practices. To align (see Chapter 7) to internal formalities requires time and effort. Moreover, externals' lack of familiarity with the context they will be operating in strains our internal capabilities, which are already engaged in averting a crisis.

Lesser sensitivity

Using the idea of lean, we could create value more efficiently but simultaneously lose the abundance, breadth and depth of internal expertise necessary to effectively manage adversity:

> Lean production can be laudable goal. A lean production organisation works to minimise waste by focusing all of its resources on producing the

best possible value for customers at the least costs. But the lean organisation can lose resilience when managers eliminate seemingly redundant positions because they also eliminate experience and expertise. This shrinks the repertoire of responses available to the organisation.

(Weick and Sutcliffe, 2015, p. 110)

Reduced adaptability

As with the previous criticism of the idea of lean, in relation to the abundant availability of expertise, the breadth and depth of management of near-misses and accidents may be reduced; fewer response options will be available that can be activated in real-time:

Resilience is about the relationship between adaptation and adaptability. In the name of efficiency, adaptation, consisting of the cost-effective use of the current resources, strips away resources that currently seem useless but could prove valuable in an altered context.

(Weick and Sutcliffe, 2015, pp. 107–108)

Lesser group cohesion

Along with our own increased emotional and structural detachment from commitment to act on impending adversity, there is also a resulting lack of group cohesion. Group cohesion is defined by feelings such as group pride or interpersonal liking, and the addition of external capacities to a group undermines the fundamental group fabric and its ability to manage the unexpected.

 ## Centrifugal wisdom

The centripetal perspective on the process of accessing proclaims the elimination of redundant capacities; it promotes the practicality and versatility of bringing in external capacities, as long as they add value. Redundancies in human resources are built up in light of potential capacity constraints and excess staff are shed when they don't create value; the risk of excess capacity is borne by the supplier.

However, the same human capacities that we may see as excessive, wasteful, or redundant are those that provide us with the mindful capabilities to withstand the fallout of near-misses and accidents. In high-reliability organisations, the build-up of seemingly redundant experience, expertise, and behaviours is purposeful:

> HROs overcome error when independent people with varied experience interdependently generate and apply a richer set of resources to a disturbance swiftly and under the guidance of negative feedback.
>
> (Weick and Sutcliffe, 2015, p. 107)

In following a strategy of redundancy in behaviours, the intent is to establish and maintain 'stand-by' capabilities that can fill the breach if we, as the owner of impending adversity, feel the need to step away from influencing it (see Chapter 6). Ergo, the centrifugal question is not about the extent to which we streamline internal and external human resources but the degree to which we build up an excess of experience and expertise (see Figure 10.4).

Figure 10.4 Building-up social redundancies.

The build-up of 'stand by' capabilities can be adjusted according to the mode in which the threat of mindless behaviours is the greatest, not in situations considered normal but in those that require an up-tempo or crisis mode of operating (Weick and Sutcliffe, 2015). In comparison with the spirit of lean, the dynamic adjustment of additional capabilities is not only value-bound but also time-bound. Excess capabilities are built up where and, most importantly, when they matter.

Investing in competencies and response repertoires

It is wise to spend money and effort building internal competencies and response repertoires. Not only do we broaden and deepen them through stretch assignments (see Chapter 5) but we also contribute to our ability and commitment to heed more warning signals (see Chapter 3). In other words, the wider our response repertoire, the greater the enhancement of our mental radar for picking up signs of impending adversity.

Keep old-timers

External newcomers may bring a fresh, new, and current perspective to the table, but they are unfamiliar with the context they need to engage with. Thus, old-timers or veterans are not to be dismissed out of hand:

> Old-timers have different experiences and competencies that are not so much out of date as they are diverse resources that may be able to cope with unexpected events.

> (Weick and Sutcliffe, 2015, p. 12)

Frontline expertise

Most often, adversity is first faced and managed by frontline employees. Hence, it is crucial to invest in frontline workers, retain them, and secure their commitment to doing their utmost best to anticipate and contain any brewing crisis (see Table 10.1).

Table 10.1 One Destination, Five Roads

	Emotional Energy Is Generated by:	Frontline Employees Commit Themselves to the Organisation because:
The Mission, Values, and Provide Path	mutual trust, collective pride, and self-discipline	they are proud of its aspirations, accomplishments, and legacy; they share its values.
The Process and Metrics Path	transparent performance measures and standards; clear tracking of results	they know what each person is expected to do, how performance is measured, and why it matters.
The Entrepreneurial Spirit Path	personal freedom, the opportunity for high earnings, and few rules about behaviour; people choose their work activities and take significant personal risks	they are in control of their own destinies; they savour the high-risk, high-reward work environment.
The Individual Achievement Path	intense respect for individual achievement in an environment with limited emphasis on personal risk and reward	they are recognised mostly for the quality of their individual performance.
The Reward and Celebration Path	recognition and celebration of organisational accomplishments	they have fun and enjoy the supportive and highly interactive environment.

Source: Adapted from Katzenbach and Santamaria, 1999, p. 4.

Group cohesion

External perspectives may well enable us to heed more warning signals (see Chapter 3), and propel us to scrutinise these warning signals (see Chapter 4); on the downside, though, they may also damage the very foundations that enable groups to engage with adversity: personal relationships and interpersonal bonds. These blossom if people are familiar with each other and are thus more likely to align with each other's actions (see Chapter 7).

The toolbox

Tiger Teams. All in all, when staring into the potential abyss of an impending crisis, bringing in additional capabilities and seeking advice from an outsider's perspective can be vital. Internal politics tend to take over in the middle of a major problem as people can become insensitive and defensive and may entrench themselves in their silos. If we want a swift solution to avert disaster, this silo mentality needs to be broken down. Tiger teams (whether they are called that or go by some other name) can deliberately be set up as high-performing teams aiming to reconcile potentially opposing views and facilitate solution-finding in out-of-control situations:

> Tiger teams are intensely managed small groups of selected experts. Their core performance comes from open and honest dialog, productive conflict, and the struggle to fit the problem pieces together to produce a unified whole.
>
> The tiger team task is problem-solving. Problem-solving consists of two sequential stages. The first stage is to define the problem: present state, goal state, and obstruction. The second stage is to find solutions: first develop all possible options, then evaluate and select.
>
> Individuals (project managers) can serve as capable analysts, working out the problem definition stage.
>
> Sometimes defining the problem is all that is necessary to solve the problem. Solution-finding, however, is best conducted by tiger teams. It is the creative solution-finding stage of project troubleshooting that managers should find most useful.
>
> (Pavlak, 2004, p. 13)

They need to be on standby or hover around a task-oriented team, monitoring the situation, and ready to provide the team with support. Tiger teams can be parachuted in when the situation warrants it. A tiger team must not replace the project manager but support the team in the following:

- Listening and asking questions from multiple perspectives about what is happening and yet not rushing to conclusions despite the pressure to act quickly.

- Imagining worst-case implications, together with the details of complex, potentially dynamically changing, tasks.

- Suppressing members' egos in terms of 'knowing the answer' yet remaining inquisitive in creating options.

- Willingness to break existing rules and processes, with the ability to think outside of the usual methods of operation.

- Skills to create solutions that work at the technical, process, and human levels.

- Ability to maintain a continuously high level of focus and intensity of action.

Maintaining all this to achieve rapid engagement with impending adversity while operating within challenging timeframes under the 'spotlight' of senior management is a demanding task. But, even then, the assignment of a tiger team does not mean they are to take over from frontline teams; instead, they should offer support in making the most informed decision possible.

Stand-by

The dynamic adjustment of capacities via outsourced resources is problematic, as the latter may not be activated in time to engage with a looming crisis marked by near-misses and accidents. Consequently, internally built social redundancies need to be on standby and able to be parachuted in real-time, to help frontline workers make a rapid transition from normal operations to up-tempo and crisis modes of operation (Weick and Sutcliffe, 2015).

Accessing - Revisiting the Afghanistan war

Of all the case studies covered in this book, one stands out as being defined by breath-taking either/or just-this-way and just-for-now thinking: the Afghan war that took place from 2001 to 2021. But it did not start as such. Following the 11th September attacks on the World Trade Centre in New York, carried out by the militant Islamist terrorist group Al-Qaeda, the United States (US) and its allies invaded Afghanistan, intending to topple the Taliban-ruled Islamic Emirate that was thought to harbour the mastermind of the 9/11 attacks: Osama bin Laden.

The invasion and early operations were successful in ousting the Taliban from power, but in 2003 the Taliban started to re-organise themselves, not least due to the US diverting its attention to another hotspot that was wrongly associated with the World Trade Centre attacks: Iraq.

From 2006 onwards, despite a multinational build-up of NATO forces (the International Security Assistance Force ISAF), the conflict became a quagmire. Places like the Korengal valley became hotly contested battle zones. Despite a troop surge in 2009, the Taliban kept on inflicting heavy casualties on Afghan security forces.

By 2011, Osama bin Laden had been killed. In 2014, with the war still at a stale-mate, it dawned on the US that it was no longer winnable. Gradually, responsi-bility for keeping the Taliban in check was transitioned to the Afghan Armed Forces. It was assumed that through training, assisting, and supporting a local force at a cost in excess of $83 billion, the Afghan Army would be enabled to repel the incessant attacks by the Taliban. However, in addition to rampant cor-ruption and a high rate of desertions, the start of peace talks in 2018 sowed doubt and suspicion among the ranks of the Afghan Armed Forces.

With the pull-out of the multinational forces, the military and police units presented a formidable force on paper only. The capital city, Kabul, was captured by the Taliban on 15th August, with little or no resistance from the Afghan Armed Forces:

> Both the Biden and Trump administrations justified their actions by present-ing a binary choice: endless combat or immediate retreat. The U.S. military, in contrast, was seeking options along that continuum — trying to find a sustainable role that would backstop the Afghan military while allowing for aggressive counterterrorism.
>
> Yet Biden, like Trump, wanted a decisive, high-profile American departure. This took a difficult, medium-term problem and turned it into a catastrophic symbol of betrayal and defeat. Decisive presidential leadership is often a virtue. In this case, living with ambiguity and watching developments might have been the better option.
>
> But the deed is done. And the Biden administration — and all that follow it — will need to deal with a brutal fact of history. Those who planned, carried out and supported the attacks of September 11th, 2001, can now claim, with some credibility, that they succeeded. Terrorists protected by the Taliban took nearly 3,000 innocent lives, caused anywhere from $2 trillion to $3 tril-lion in economic damage and encouraged a generation of American recrimi-nation and self-doubt, all for about $500,000 — the money it took to mount the operation.

(Gerson, 2021)

Just-this-way and just-for-now

With a crisis imminent, we long for additional capacities to bolster our defences, particularly under circumstances where our own resources are scarce. Just-this-way (see Figure 10.5), we draw on seemingly dispensable external capacities. In the case of Afghanistan, NATO forces never had the necessary potential to pacify vast swathes of rural territory:

> We can't win the war in Afghanistan, so what do we do? We'll train the Afghans to do it for us, then claim victory and head for the exits.
>
> But what happens if we can't train the Afghans?

> (Filkins, 2012)

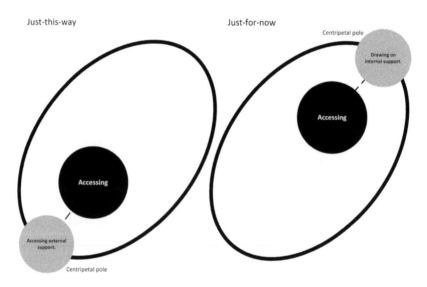

Figure 10.5 Just-this-way and just-for-now polarity (accessing).

In contrast to the strict dependence on external capacities, we may consider, just-for-now, the opposite. Beyond the surge of troops in 2009, NATO would have had to deploy a multitude of troops on the ground to effectively keep the Taliban, who most often relied on hit-and-run tactics, in check. The quantity of NATO-provided internal capacity needed just to retain control, let alone the quantity of capacity needed to engage with the Taliban fully and eventually defeat them, would have been enormous. So in principle, both just-this-way and just-for-now poles, if overused, appear nonsensical.

Just-in-case and just-in-time

We are focused on cutting our losses or failure to manage adversity by relying on external support. This may provide us with additional capacity to deal with any eventuality. On the other hand, building up internal support provides us with rapid access to mindsets that are familiar with the context in question.

As in all the previous chapters, it is less a question of either/or, and more one of both/and (see Figure 10.6). In the case of the Afghan war, it is one of adding external capacity as well as integrating it into a unified whole (see Chapter 7):

> The three imperatives that exemplify our commitment and urgency to this mission are: "Team, Transparency, and Transition." To change the dynamics in Afghanistan we must team with the Afghan Ministries and security forces to develop their capabilities to provide security. We must develop transparent, enduring, and self-sustaining processes to generate, educate, train, and employ professional and effective security forces. By teaming with the Afghans, we will develop their capabilities and thereby transition the security responsibility for Afghanistan to national security forces that can protect the population and safeguard their nation.
>
> (Combined Security Transition Command, 2010)

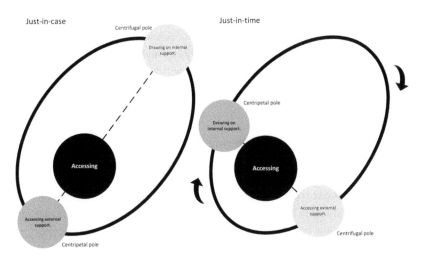

Figure 10.6 Just-in-case and just-in-time polarity (accessing).

Just-in-time, a dynamic adjustment could have involved a greater emphasis on external support through Afghan Military Forces, with NATO in the background, serving as a gigantic tiger team on standby, to be parachuted in when necessary.

This dynamic adjustment, though, was undermined by the relatively sudden and stark decision to withdraw NATO forces from the Afghan theatre.

Let's define some guiding both/and principles that may have averted such a disaster:

JUST-IN-CASE, we are reluctant to rely on external capacities WHILE building up our own. In light of the infinite, supposedly insurmountable adversity that we face (see Chapter 6), we are bent on adding additional capacities that can be shed instantly. Then, while we are concentrating our effort on protecting our core activities and functions, we invest and train our internal capacities.

JUST-IN-CASE, we are tempted to fall back on external capacities WHILE integrating them. We may not just add external support to our management of impending adversity, but also align it (Chapter 7) with our workings. That includes not just making these external capacities mindlessly go through to-do lists; instead, we fully integrate their support into unified ownership of impending adversity. That requires transparency and openness towards each other's way of working and the commitment to a collective, bigger picture.

The previous two guiding principles may come across as very static as if we set these in stone regardless of changes in our circumstances. Let's add a temporal condition:

JUST-IN-TIME, we are reluctant to rely on external capacities WHILE building up our own AS LONG AS we can parachute these internal resources in quickly. As long as we can build up our own internal capacities, expand them, invest in them, and access them, we are reluctant to add external resources to the mix. Only once we have identified that our internal support is becoming inaccessible and over-stretched do we ready ourselves to integrate additional external capacities.

Towards a paradox mindset

Although we are drawn towards bringing in external additions to help us in being task-oriented towards preventing and containing looming adversity, such outside capacity may do more harm than good as it adds additional challenges. And yet, gaining an external perspective – looking at adversity from the opposite pole – is helpful in managing impending adversity:

Every once in a while, an outsider comes along with a new vision or a new way of doing things that revolutionises a scientific field, an industry, or a culture. Take the case of Katalin Karikó, who defied all odds to pioneer the mRNA technology that ultimately gave the world Covid-19 vaccines in record time. Daughter of a butcher and raised in a small adobe house in the former Eastern bloc with no running water or refrigerator, Karikó started working with RNA as a student in Hungary but moved to the United States in her late twenties. For decades, she faced rejection after rejection, the scorn of colleagues, and even the threat of deportation. Yet today, Karikó's foundational work on mRNA is at the heart of the vaccines developed by BioNTech/Pfizer and Moderna, and many researchers are now calling for Karikó to win the Nobel Prize.

(Cattani and Ferriani, 2021)

References

Ainslie, G. and Haslam, N. (1992) 'Hyperbolic discounting', in Loewenstein, G. and Elster, J. (eds.) *Choice over time*. New York: Russel Sage Foundation, pp. 57–92.

Cattani, G. and Ferriani, S. (2021) *How outsiders become game changers, Harvard Business Review*. Available at: https://hbr.org/2021/08/how-outsiders-become-game-changers.

Combined Security Transition Command (2010) 'Nato Training Mission APO AE 09356'. Kabul: NTM-A/CSTC-A-CG.

Earl, M. J. (1996) 'The risks of outsourcing IT', *MIT Sloan Management Review*, 37, pp. 26–32.

Filkins, D. (2012) *The definition of a Quagmire, The New Yorker*. Available at: https://www.newyorker.com/news/news-desk/the-definition-of-a-quagmire.

Gerson, M. (2021) *Forever war vs. hasty retreat: Afghanistan didn't have to be a binary choice, The Washington Post*. Available at: https://www.washingtonpost.com/opinions/2021/08/30/afghanistan-forever-war-vs-quick-retreat-not-binary-choice/.

Kahneman, D. and Lovallo, D. (2003) 'Delusions of success: How optimism undermines executives' decisions', *Harvard Business Review*, 81(7), pp. 56–63.

Kahneman, D. and Tversky, A. (1991) 'Loss aversion in riskless choice: A reference-dependent model', *The Quarterly Journal of Economics*, 106(4), pp. 1039–1061.

Katzenbach, J. R. and Santamaria, J. A. (1999) 'Firing up the front line', *Harvard Business Review*, 77(3), pp. 107–119.

Pavlak, A. (2004) 'Project troubleshooting: Tiger teams for reactive risk management', *Project Management Journal*, 35(4), pp. 5–14.

Project Management Institute (2022) *The five principles of Lean*. Available at: https://www.pmi.org/disciplined-agile/lean/principles.

Samuelson, W. and Zeckhauser, R. (1988) 'Status quo bias in decision making', *Journal of Risk and Uncertainty*, 1(1), pp. 7–59.

Weick, K. and Sutcliffe, K. (2015) *Managing the unexpected: Sustained performance in a complex world*. 3rd edn. Hoboken, NJ: Wiley.

Womack, J. P. and Jones, D. T. (1994) 'From lean production to the lean enterprise', *Harvard Business Review*, 72(2), pp. 93–103.

Chapter 11

Mindful organising through paradoxical thinking

Navigating the roads to resilience

Our longing for solutions to impending adversity is often characterised by monolithic, deterministic, and reductionist thinking. Based on our past successes and failures, we reduce our thinking to just-this-way (see Figure 11.1), to answers we can quickly activate in order to anticipate and contain the ramifications of near-misses and accidents. Why should we start from a different angle and think of the preposterous alternative of taking the opposite pole into account? Only if just-this-way does not work out may we be tempted to try out the opposite of what we have been doing. Even if, as a just-for-now measure, the opposite of what we are used to thinking is right can provide us with an alternative, ostensive angle, we cannot stick with it for long because we have not set the scene for its performative realisation.

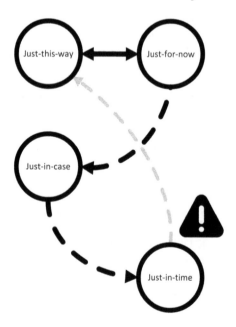

Figure 11.1 From just-this-way to just-in-time.

DOI: 10.4324/9781003083115-11

The lure of
just-this-
way and
just-for-now
leadership

So, we may constantly pivot between the monolithic poles of just-this-way and just-for-now, getting frustrated with the overuse of an either/or mentality. To break out of either/or thinking, we may need a push to help us advance beyond just-this-way and just-for-now approaches by appreciating and integrating an opposite pole, angle, or perspective that in isolation may look absurd, but which, when integrated, provides us with alternative, opportunistic third ways of preventing the materialisation of a looming crisis.

The push for both/and just-in-case thinking provides us with answers that take advantage of the benefits of both poles but unfortunately also bring to the forefront tensions of polar incompatibility. In other words, we may try to integrate both poles, but in effect, that generates more disbenefits than benefits in managing adversity; the paradoxical fallout should not be discounted.

Notwithstanding the paradoxical feedback loops, we may define guiding just-in-case principles where the benefits of integrating polar extremes outweigh polarity tensions. It is then a further challenge not to treat these principles as static, constant, immovable, and stationary; instead, they need to be dynamically adjusted and adapted depending on the context we find ourselves in: just-in-time.

The lure of just-this-way and just-for-now leadership

When we think of leadership, we may draw on the traditional notion of a leader holding a position of power, rank, and status, exhibiting strength and decisiveness in making decisions that others follow and realise. All efforts to define goals, objectives and directions, take action and manage adversity stem from that leader.

The lure of following a just-this-way leader (see Figure 11.2) is straightforward:

> Old ways die hard. Amid all the evidence that our world is radically changing, we cling to what has worked in the past. We still think of organisations in mechanistic terms, as collections of replaceable parts capable of being reengineered. We act as if even people were machines, redesigning their jobs as we would prepare an engineering diagram, expecting them to perform to specifications with machine like obedience. Over the years, our ideas of leadership have supported this metaphoric myth. We sought prediction and control, and also charged leaders with providing everything that was absent from the machine: vision, inspiration, intelligence, and courage. They alone had to provide the energy and direction to move their rusting vehicles of organisation into the future.

(Wheatley, 1997, p. 21)

189

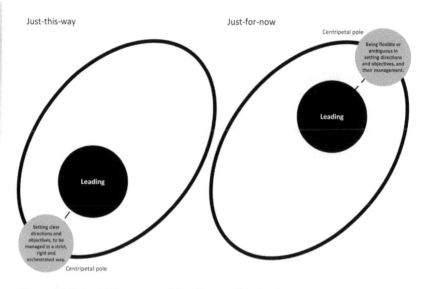

Figure 11.2 Just-this-way and just-for-now leadership.

It is not surprising that such command and control leadership is still commonplace, as it provides a perception of clarity, directness, accuracy, precision, consistency, and determinism in managing future adversity (Roe and Schulman, 2008). Nevertheless, reliance on such a leadership style comes at a price:

> … there is no best way to do anything independent of context, so the leader cannot have privileged information. When leaders keep everyone in their place with the illusion of knowability and possession of this privileged knowledge the benefit to them is that we "obey" and leaders feel superior. The cost is that they create lemmings. Their mindlessness promotes our own mindlessness which costs us our well being and health. Net result, the leader, the led, and the company all lose.
>
> (Langer, 2010)

Against that temptation to give in to the centripetal notion of rather mindless leadership (see Figure 11.2), the opposite pole to traditional leadership is one of flexibility and allowing ambiguity to flourish:

> In high reliability management, ambiguity can be a strength. Much is accomplished by good judgement rather than explicit instructions. Ambiguity allows discretion and protects against error in explicit commands.
>
> (Roe and Schulman, 2008, p. 150)

And yet, if overused, such discretion results in doubt, vagueness, imprecision, and indecision. Just as with all other constructs that we deem salient in managing adversity, it is not a question of either/or but one of both/and.

The toolbox

The tools covered in this book help us to make sense of simultaneous opposites and to take actions to anticipate and respond to near-misses and accidents. Nonetheless, we cannot give meaning to polarities if we do not know what they are. So a very useful tool to understand polarities is the repertory grid interview technique:

Repertory grid. For the study that shaped this book (see Chapter 1), the interview technique of repertory grid was motivated by the need to uncover the implicit, tacit, and deep-seated belief systems of managers that they draw on to anticipate and respond to near-misses and accidents:

> Managers often erect defence mechanisms that oversimplify the complexity of the seemingly contradictory tensions with simple either/or options. This implies that they do not give much thought to broadening their alternatives. Training managers to think more deeply about how they think about organisational paradoxes using the grid technique grounded in the psychology of personal constructs holds the promise of developing more "complicated understanding" that goes beyond normal logic and open access to other forms of reasoning.
>
> (Wright, 2020, p. 318)

A repertory grid interview may be amended to suit the needs of the subject in question. Once completed, it provides a robust and rigorous method to uncover aspects of bipolarity:

> Grids are very powerful, and for two reasons, the first of which you can anticipate already. They allow people to express their views by means of their own constructs, not yours – in other words, to talk about the world in their own terms. No one can object that someone else's assumptions have been laid on them; no one has put words into the person's mouth. I'm sure you can think of many situations in which this is desirable.
>
> Secondly, once you as the investigator have discovered a person's constructs, the person's own terms of reference, the grid will allow you to identify exactly what the other person means when s/he uses those terms. Each element is rated on each construct, to provide an

191

exact picture of what the person wishes to say about each element within a topic.

Between them, the elements, constructs, and ratings of elements on constructs provide you with a kind of mental map: a precise statement of the way in which the individual thinks of, gives meaning to, construes, the topic in question.

(Jankowicz, 2004, pp. 13–14)

The need for just-in-case and just-in-time leadership

Not only do we need to be 'pushed' away from just-this-way and just-for-now paradoxes, due to the inadequate overuse of monolithic reasoning, but we are also 'pulled' towards just-in-case and just-in-time thinking (Roe and Schulman, 2008). These contextual pull forces are defined by coupling and interactions (see Figure 11.3).

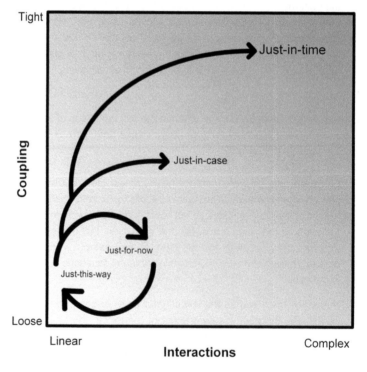

Figure 11.3 Coupling and interactions (adapted from Perrow, 1999).

The environmental aspect of loose coupling implies that points of failure or deviations from a planned state are relatively independent, and buffers or slack between them can limit the effects of interconnectivity. Loose coupling provides time for 'breathing space' to contain failures, and they can often be addressed individually, thereby preventing them from gradually destabilising the whole. In a tightly coupled system, such as a nuclear power plant (Perrow, 1999), interdependencies between elements mean that incidents can build upon themselves and escalate rapidly. In this respect, complexity prompts us to implement practices that provide speedy interventions, even more so in environments characterised by tight coupling.

A complex system is further associated with a lack of predictable, visible, familiar, or comprehensible interactions. In a nuclear power plant, for instance, this means operators facing uncertainty: for example, being unable to diagnose and thus respond properly to the unplanned automatic shutdown of the reactor. Given the tensions and their management, as described, each mode of resilience offers different benefits dependent upon the expected coupling and interactions (Perrow, 1999).

In correspondence with the degree of interaction and coupling, we may pivot between just-this-way and just-for-now as long as we perceive the context we are operating in as loose and linear. We may have entrenched thinking, just-this-way, but also have the time and space to shift towards the opposite extreme, just-for-now.

Unfortunately, most of the environments we deal with are anything but linear and loose; instead, they are complex and tight. Assuming that they are, we need to have paradoxical capabilities that enable us to strike a fine balance between setting clear directions and realising them in a strict, rigid, and orchestrated way while being flexible or ambiguous about those self-same directions and objectives (see Figure 11.4) in real-time.

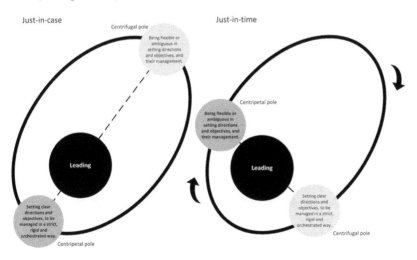

Figure 11.4 Just-this-case and just-in-time leadership.

193

The aspect of real-time, just-in-time, is vital. Under tight coupling conditions, we need to rebalance the tension-laden juxtaposition of centripetal and centrifugal leadership quickly to prevent the occurrence of near-misses and accidents and their cascade into crisis and irrecoverable disaster. Roe and Schulman (2008, p. 136) summarise the pull factors towards just-in-time as follows:

1. Real-time is an answer to persistent network incompleteness.
2. Positive interdependencies are most evident and likely to be acted on in real-time.
3. Real-time remains informal, nonroutine, and flexible.
4. Real-time allows for larger process variance relative to output variance around the balance of load and generation.
5. Real-time legitimates and accommodates the redefining of reliability criteria.
6. Real-time operations justify and reward improvisation and experimentation.

So, where does this leave us in leading the effort to manage adversity? We are being pushed and pulled to embrace just-in-case thinking and to be ready to adjust these third-way balances of bipolarity dynamically, in real-time. That is by no means an easy feat, so we need some support in the form of tools.

The toolbox

A review. The repertory grid interview technique or equivalent method provides a deep dive into the world of simultaneous opposites that we draw on to make sense of, for example, managing impending adversity. There are some useful tools that help to make sense of simultaneous opposites and the associated tensions between bipolar constructs that are both complementary and contradictory.

Polarity mapping. The most prominent tool is the polarity map, conceived by Barry Johnson (1996). As shown in Figure 11.5, the following process may be followed:

1. Pole names – Create names for each of the poles.
2. Benefits and overuses – Differentiate the poles by identifying the good things the pole brings as well as the problems that arise when there is too much of it.
3. The transformational Third Way – Reintegrate the poles by identifying what they look like when harmonised.
4. The vulnerability throughway – Identify the risks and the courage needed to step into the tension that creates the Third Way.
5. Strategies – Brainstorm and decide on actions to navigate the polarity from the Third Way over time (Emerson and Lewis, 2019, p. 56).

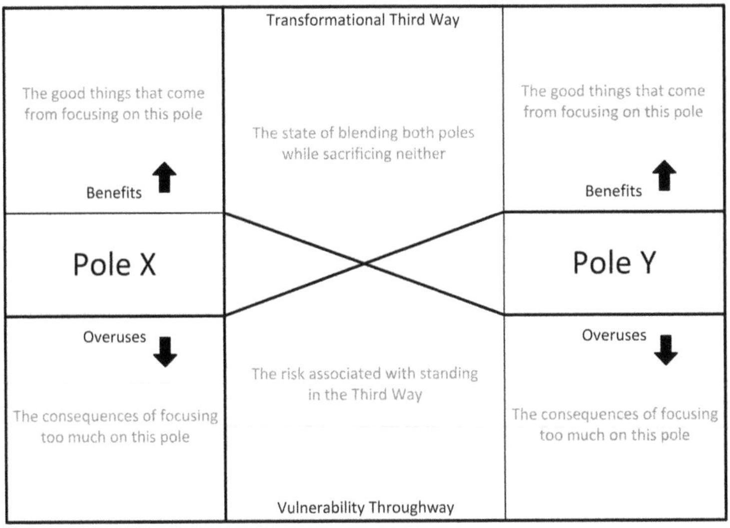

	Transformational Third Way	
The good things that come from focusing on this pole	The state of blending both poles while sacrificing neither	The good things that come from focusing on this pole
Benefits ↑		Benefits ↑
Pole X		**Pole Y**
Overuses ↓		Overuses ↓
The consequences of focusing too much on this pole	The risk associated with standing in the Third Way	The consequences of focusing too much on this pole
	Vulnerability Throughway	

Figure 11.5 Polarity map (adapted from Emerson and Lewis, 2019, p. 55).

In addition to polarity mapping, there are other tools already covered in this book that allow us to appreciate opposites and contrasts, contradictions and paradoxes, and likeness, agreements, and sameness. They can be used in conjunction with polarity mapping:

Benefits mapping. As introduced in Chapter 2, Benefits mapping outlines the activities necessary for achieving the planned benefits. Nevertheless, there may be disbenefits within these relationships that run contrary to our need to follow the benefits roadmap. A polarity map may enable us to identify and explore the enablers and changes required to realise benefits.

Scenario planning and pre-mortem. Scenario planning (see Chapter 3) makes us a model and thinks about extreme futures: reasonable worst- and best-case scenarios and in-between scenarios. A pre-mortem facilitates better approaches to worst cases and further identifies threats, weaknesses, and vulnerabilities that make a worst-case scenario more likely. In addition to scenario planning and a pre-mortem, polarity mapping helps us to critically dissect how to prevent a pre-mortemed worst-case scenario and pursue a best-case outcome.

Four ways of seeing and Socratic questioning. Four ways of seeing and Socratic questioning (see Chapter 4) counter the temptation to oversimplify by taking other perspectives into account and by raising questions that would not otherwise be raised. The mapping of polarities may further help us understand these perspectives and how they align with ours.

Culpability and counterfactual analysis. The question of culpability can be informed by carrying out a counterfactual analysis (see Chapter 6). Testing cause-and-effect relationships under a variety of conditions may be enhanced through mapping polarities. 'What if?' cause-effect relationships can be further analysed by exploring tensions of bipolar just-in-case and just-in-time actions.

Just-in-time reconstruction of managing near-misses and accidents

Throughout this book, you may have wondered why near-misses and accidents are treated similarly. Both types of incidents provide valuable data to inform interventive and corrective action. If near-misses are contained, we prevent significant consequences from materialising. Nevertheless, near-misses are more difficult to pick up because of the lack of detectable and evident ramifications:

> Learning from past events is complicated by the hindsight bias – the tendency, after the fact, to overestimate the amount of information one thought relevant at the time a decision was made (Fischhoff, 1975; Fischhoff and Beyth, 1975; Gephart, 1993). Thus, the hindsight bias suggests that only after a catastrophe do people see the warnings embedded in near-miss events.

> (Dillon and Tinsley, 2008, p. 1426)

Although we tend to pay more attention to events that leave a lasting impact on us or our organisation, should we not be more mindful about otherwise 'unseen' near-misses?

Making us 'see' near-misses will require us to focus on constructs (see Figure 11.6) that enable us to anticipate them: heeding, simplifying, clarifying, and engaging. In order to contain accidents and prevent them from snowballing into disasters, we concentrate our efforts on: aligning, following, influencing, deferring, and accessing.

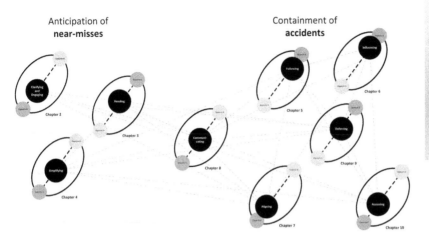

Figure 11.6 Constructs priority.

The toolbox

Construct coaching. We, as high-reliability professionals, may use the tools mentioned above to help us and others understand the bipolar construct system we draw on to make sense of the tensions we face. We do not have to engage with a sophisticated interview technique such as repertory grid to do this but can instead rely on simpler tools such as polarity mapping.

As construct coaches, we provide others with *"methodological support"* (Pavlovic and Stojnov, 2020, p. 323) as a means of bringing forth a *"temporary resolution of the inherent paradoxes of their lived experiences"* (Wright, 2020, p. 307) by drawing on the following process.

Exploring bipolar opposites

The first step in the process of facilitating (Stojnov and Pavlovic, 2010) the self of a manager, the construct coach, explores the manager's preferred and non-preferred realities of learning (Pavlovic and Stojnov, 2020). As managers, we may be inherently incapable of articulating such realities; therefore, techniques such as repertory grid interviews (Jankowicz, 2004) or polarity mapping (e.g. Johnson, 1996) may be used to explore the tacit construct systems defined by centripetal and centrifugal poles.

Exploring tensions and facilitating conversations

The reconstruction of a bipolar construct system will then be fine-tuned (Stojnov and Pavlovic, 2010), as displayed in Figure 11.7.

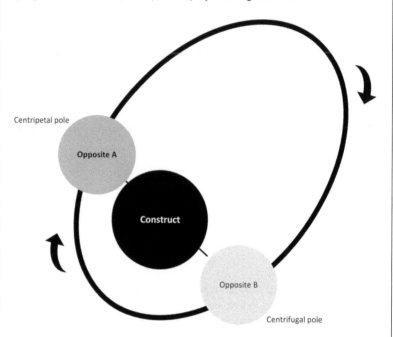

Centripetal pole

Opposite A

Construct

Opposite B

Centrifugal pole

Figure 11.7 From just-this-way to just-in-time.

We may be engaged with overemphasis and overuse of the centripetal pole associated with anticipation and response relating to near-misses and accidents. The evaluation and appreciation of the advantages of the under-emphasised centrifugal pole may produce a reconfiguration of how centripetal and centrifugal forces solidify the core definition of a learning process core construct. For example, despite our gravitation towards a particular centripetal pole, we may perceive a deficiency in the opposite one due to our action; we can take steps to correct that by complementing the preferred pole with its opposite.

Experimentation and evaluation

After conceptualising the implications of a reconstructed experience, we may then *"reflect-in-action"* (Schoen, 1983). Such reflection may be loosely associated with what Kelly (1955) described as fixed role therapy. As part of this *"try on for size"* (Pavlovic and Stojnov, 2020, p. 325) exercise, we are asked to enact a new character, a new version of ourselves in *"one good, rousing, construct-shaking experience"* (Kelly, 1955, p. 412). In the form of a role-play, simulation or experiment, the experience may result in the emergence of further tacit constructs that could constrain our ability to resolve centripetal and centrifugal forces. It may reveal paradoxical aspects that make a temporary resolution of paradoxical tensions untenable, meaning that we have to go back to our starting point. Questions that can aid the preparation and facilitation of the experienced 'as if' enactment include the following:

• What could be done differently in the particular situation?

• Can you imagine a scenario where you would act differently?

• What would happen if you behaved differently?

• What stops you from doing it? (Stojnov and Pavlovic, 2010, p. 136)

The stages of construct reconstruction represent a continuous, evaluative process that addresses the dynamic nature of centripetal and centrifugal forces. This process should not permanently transform our belief system if it collides with the normative, professional desires of our work unit. And it should not just result in more (albeit different) monolithic, dogmatic auto-pilot thinking. Instead, it should continuously free our minds towards dualities.

 ## Establishing a culture of mindful, paradoxical organising

Formerly, leadership was circumscribed by specific characteristics we associate with ourselves and others. And yet,

> Leadership is really not about leaders themselves. It's about a collective practice among people who work together – accomplishing the choices we make together in our mutual work.

(Raelin, 2015)

Such collective practice is embedded, facilitated, and constrained within cultures that are made up of assumptions, values, identities, and beliefs about how we behave and interact and what practices and routines we adhere to. Our culture defines the unwritten customs, rules, etiquettes, traditions, and established ways of doing things in our work unit. In the words of Schein (2011, p. 313), culture is:

1. a pattern of shared basic assumptions,
2. invented, discovered, or developed by a given group,

3. as it learns to cope with its problems of external adaptation and internal integration,
4. that has worked well enough to be considered valid, and therefore, is to be taught to new members of the group as the correct way to perceive, think, and feel in relation to these problems.

To cultivate an organisational paradox mindset, we may think of sharing values such as creativity, being open-minded, and having the courage to experiment with the opposite of what is traditionally valued. We may even go so far as to embrace the absurd by looking for and dwelling on it. Such values of open-mindedness could, paradoxically, challenge the very foundation we rely on: an established and shared set of values.

> In organisations, people interpret and contest values all the time. In my university, one of the core values espoused is responsibility, which is defined as meaning "to serve as a catalyst for positive change in Texas and beyond." This definition is quite different from my own. I associated the word "responsibility" with accountability and duty, rather than with being a catalyst for change. Also, how does one define positive change? I suspect it is quite different from one member of the university community to another. Even if most members of the university agree that responsibility is an important value, many may not agree with what that means or feel that the stated definition represents their own ideas about responsibility.
>
> To further complicate things, people may contest "common" values while maintaining their commitment to the success of the organisation. This may be as obvious as open disagreement, or as subtle as a manager quietly reshaping a project to reflect their personal ideas about how things should be done. It could show up as a tacit rise in absenteeism or overt complaints about decisions made by leaders. Indeed, one might complain about the decisions of leaders precisely because one is committed to the organisation and feels that the direction that leadership is moving in is wrong.
>
> (Traphagan, 2017, p. 3)

This implies that whatever culture we seek to establish in order to foster paradoxical thinking will itself be constantly questioned, challenged, and contested. The resulting tensions should not be resolved by either/or but with processes to manage impending adversity. The answers can only be a provisional, short-lived both/and.

We, as high-reliability professionals

So, where does that leave us as high-reliability professionals? Are we supposed to impose our way of managing impending adversity on others mindlessly? Or are we looking at the opposite? Do we seek a both/and definition of managing the unexpected, depending on the context we are in? Given that the future remains uncertain and complex, we are repeatedly pulled towards just-in-time mindful organising (see Figure 11.8).

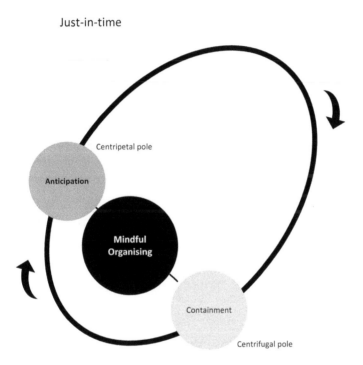

Figure 11.8 Just-in-time mindful organising.

Our job is to create *"a combined cognitive space"* (Roe and Schulman, 2008, p. 121) that allows us to navigate the bipolarity of processes we deem salient to managing near-miss incidents and accidents. We are construct coaches who collectively reconstruct our complex construct systems dynamically so that we are ready to engage with a multitude of interactive and coupled environments.

However, we need to be careful. On one hand, that cognitive space that allows us to think about both/and third ways with a very limited shelf-life is constantly under threat; we may be pressured by a deadline and so go back to what is quicker: either/or. On the other hand, on the opposite extreme, the overuse of mindful, paradoxical organising could result in cognitive overload, leading to paralysis by analysis. Our longing for the ideal both/and sweet spot may stop us in our tracks while the environment around us keeps on changing.

Any yet, think like Einstein:

> Harvard University psychiatrist Albert Rothenberg was among the first to investigate the idea formally, with a study in 1996 of acclaimed geniuses. Interviewing 22 Nobel laureates, and analysing historical accounts of deceased world-changing scientists, he noted that each revolutionary thinker had spent considerable time "actively conceiving multiple opposites or antitheses simultaneously".
>
> Einstein, for instance, contemplated how an object could be both at rest and moving depending on the position of the observer, a consideration that ultimately led to his relativity theory. Danish physicist Niels Bohr tried to reconcile the ways that energy acted like both waves and particles: states that existed simultaneously, even though they could not be observed together. This train of thought ultimately inspired a startling new understanding of quantum mechanics.
>
> (Heracleous and Robson, 2020)

Happy navigating!

 References

Dillon, R. L. and Tinsley, C. H. (2008) 'How near-misses influence decision making under risk: A missed opportunity for learning', *Management Science*, 54(8), pp. 1425–1440.

Emerson, B. and Lewis, K. (2019) *Navigating polarities: Using both/and thinking to lead transformation*. Washington, DC: Paradoxical Press.

Fischhoff, B. (1975) 'Hindsight = Foresight: The effect of outcome knowledge on judgment under uncertainty', *Journal of Experimental Psychology: Human Perception and Performance*, 1(3), pp. 288–299.

Fischhoff, B. and Beyth, R. (1975) '"I knew it would happen". Remembered probabilities of once future things', *Organizational Behavior and Human Performance*, 13(1), pp. 1–16.

Gephart, R. P. (1993) 'The textual approach: Risk and blame in disaster sensemaking', *Academy of Management Journal*, 36(6), pp. 1465–1514.

Heracleous, L. and Robson, D. (2020) *Why the 'paradox mindset' is the key to success*, *Worklife*. Available at: https://www.bbc.com/worklife/article/20201109-why-the-paradox-mindset-is-the-key-to-success.

Jankowicz, D. (2004) *The easy guide to repertory grids*. Chichester: John Wiley & Sons, Inc.

Johnson, B. (1996) *Polarity management: Identifying and managing unsolvable problems*. Amherst: HRD Press.

Kelly, G. A. (1955) *The psychology of personal constructs*. New York: Norton.

Langer, E. J. (2010) *A call for mindful leadership*, *Harvard Business Review*. Available at: https://hbr.org/2010/04/leaders-time-to-wake-up.

Lewis, M. W., Andriopoulos, C. and Smith, W. K. (2014) 'Paradoxical leadership to enable strategic agility', *California Management Review*, 56(3), pp. 58–77.

Pavlovic, J. and Stojnov, D. (2020) 'Personal construct coaching', in Winter, D. and Reed, N. (eds) *The Wiley handbook of personal construct psychology*. Hoboken, NJ: Wiley-Blackwell, pp. 320–329.

Perrow, C. (1999) *Normal accidents: Living with high-risk technologies*. Princeton, NJ: Princeton University Press.

Raelin, J. A. (2015) 'Rethinking leadership', *MIT Sloan Management Review*, 56(4), pp. 96–97.

Roe, E. and Schulman, P. R. (2008) *High reliability management: Operating on the edge*. Stanford, CA: Stanford University Press.

Schein, E. H. (2011) 'What is culture?', in Gittell, J. H. and Godwyn, M. (eds) *Sociology of organizations: Structures and relationships*. Thousand Oaks, CA: Sage Publications, pp. 311–314.

Schoen, D. (1983) *The reflective practitioner: How professionals think in action*. New York: Basic Books.

Stojnov, D. and Pavlovic, J. (2010) 'Invitation to personal construct coaching', *Invitation to Personal Construct Coaching*, 5(2), pp. 129–139.

Traphagan, J. (2017) 'We're thinking about organizational culture all wrong', *Harvard Business Review*, January 6, pp. 2–4.

Wheatley, M. (1997) 'Goodbye, command and control', *Leader to Leader*, 5(3), pp. 21–28.

Wright, R. (2020) 'Organizational Paradoxes - When Opposites cease to be Opposites', in Winter, D. and Reed, N. (eds) *The Wiley Handbook of Personal Construct Psychology*. Hoboken, New Jersey: Wiley-Blackwell.

Index

Note: **Bold** page numbers refer to tables and *italic* page numbers refer to figures.

Ingram Content Group UK Ltd.
Milton Keynes UK
UKHW011509140523
421689UK00019B/149